Trackers
Teacher's Guide

Elephant
Trackers
Level 1

Frog
Trackers
Level 2

KATE RUTTLE
Series Editor

OXFORD
UNIVERSITY PRESS

UNIVERSITY PRESS

Great Clarendon Street, Oxford OX2 6DP

Oxford University Press is a department of the University of Oxford.
It furthers the University's objective of excellence in research,
scholarship, and education by publishing worldwide in

Oxford New York

Auckland Cape Town Dar es Salaam Hong Kong Karachi
Kuala Lumpur Madrid Melbourne Mexico City Nairobi
New Delhi Shanghai Taipei Toronto

With offices in

Argentina Austria Brazil Chile Czech Republic France
Greece Guatemala Hungary Italy Japan Poland Portugal
Singapore South Korea Switzerland Thailand Turkey
Ukraine Vietnam

Oxford is a registered trade mark of Oxford University Press
in the UK and in certain other countries

Text copyright © Kate Ruttle 2004

Illustrations copyright © Oxford University Press 2004

The moral rights of the author have been asserted

Database right Oxford University Press (maker)

First published 2004

British Library Cataloguing in Publication Data

Data available

ISBN: 978-0-19-838380-2

10 9 8 7

Illustrations by Jane Bottomley, Susan Hutchison and Tony Linsell

Typeset by Fakenham Photosetting, Fakenham, Norfolk

Printed in Great Britain by Ashford Colour Press Ltd, Gosport, Hants

Acknowledgements

As authors of the *Trackers* series, we would like to thank the many 'behind the scenes' people who
have worked so hard to make this project such fun. In particular we owe thanks to the talented and
industrious team at Oxford University Press whose enthusiasm and dedication to all aspects of the
project has been unwavering and infectious. We are also extremely grateful for the skill and hard
work of the freelance people we have been lucky enough to work with, including editors Annemarie
Young and Anne Priestley, and designers Lauren Foster and James Arnold.

Trackers has been trialled in many different schools around England and we are grateful for all the
enthusiastic feedback from the teachers and children. Special thanks go to the West Oxford
Community School. We have also benefited hugely from advice from literacy consultants and
University Departments of Education around the UK, in particular Sue Ellis (Department of Primary
Education, University of Strathclyde) and Tessa Knott. Thank you everybody for your comments. We
have read and discussed them all and your feedback has helped us to make the books even better!

Sarah Fleming, Paul Shipton and Kate Ruttle

Contents

Introduction

The *Trackers* series of books is a carefully structured non-fiction and fiction reading resource for children aged 7+ who have a reading age of 5+. The books are particularly suitable for children who:

★ are finding reading a struggle,
★ are reluctant to read, or
★ are acquiring English as an additional language.

The two main aims of *Trackers* are:

★ to provide motivating 'must read' books with an interest age of 7+ and which matches the conceptual development of these children, while having a reading age of 5+;
★ to develop children's comprehension skills through generating an expectation that reading is concerned with 'getting meaning off the page', using a variety of strategies and cueing systems.

Trackers components and levels

Trackers level	National Curriculum level	Interest age	Pupil reading books	Teaching material
1 Elephant tracks	England & Wales – 1B Scotland – working within level A N. Ireland – working towards level 2	7+ years	6 non-fiction (16pp) 4 fiction (16pp)	Teacher's Guide for levels 1 and 2
2 Frog tracks	England & Wales – 1A/B Scotland – working within level A N. Ireland – working towards level 2	7+ years	6 non-fiction (16pp) 4 fiction (16pp)	Guided Reading Booklet for every title
3 Giraffe tracks	England & Wales – 1A Scotland – working towards level B N. Ireland – working within level 2	8+ years	6 non-fiction (16pp) 4 fiction (16pp)	Teacher's Guide for levels 3 and 4
4 Parrot tracks	England & Wales – 1A/2C Scotland – working towards level B N. Ireland – working within level 2	8+ years	6 non-fiction (24pp) 4 fiction (24pp)	Guided Reading Booklet for every title
5 Tiger tracks	England & Wales – 2C Scotland – working within level B N. Ireland – working within level 2	9+ years	6 non-fiction (24pp) 4 fiction (24pp)	Teacher's Guide for levels 5 and 6
6 Zebra tracks	England & Wales – 2B Scotland – working within level B N. Ireland – working within level 2	9+ years	6 non-fiction (24pp) 4 fiction (24pp)	Guided Reading Booklet for every title

How do Trackers differ from books designed for younger children?

By the time children are 7+, they will have had previous experience of reading, albeit not always successful. This means that *Trackers* can make assumptions that children understand how reading 'works' (for example the eye-movement is from left to right across the page; book language has its own conventions; readers have different expectations of fiction and non-fiction books). *Trackers* books differ from books whose target audience is children aged 4+ in a number of key ways:

★ All the books look like books for older children; they are not printed in a large font with very simple illustrations but have age appropriate illustrations and are printed in a variety of appropriately sized typefaces.

★ *Trackers* books are designed to grab the reader's attention and to make the children want to read and re-read them. Given that many children in the target audience have not found reading to be a rewarding experience, *Trackers* books work extra hard to provide that added incentive.

★ The design of each book is varied to suit the contents of the book. This is consistent with other books in the 7+ classroom.

★ The non-fiction books look like other non-fiction books available in school and class libraries. For instance, they make use of more sophisticated information presentation devices like simple charts, graphs and tables, and the text is not consistently placed on all pages.

★ The non-fiction books include real, 'new' information that is age appropriate. Many non-fiction books for younger children won't add to older children's general knowledge – *Trackers* will!

★ The fiction story lines are more sophisticated than those used in the early stages of 'traditional' reading schemes and are aimed at the more mature humour and understanding of the slightly older child.

★ The books are longer than comparable books in traditional reading schemes and there is more text on the page. Since we are providing books for older children, the traditional eight-page 'small books for small hands' approach is unnecessary, as is the idea that there should

only be one line of text on a page. If the text is accessible and interesting, older children can cope with two or three lines of text, even in the very earliest stages, and often need this quantity of text to give a good 'run in' so that comprehension strategies will work.

Are different Trackers titles aimed at children in particular year groups?

No. *Trackers* are aimed at any child aged between about 7 and 12 whose reading attainment matches the book. The reading profile on page 96 will give more guidance as to which *Trackers* level a child is best suited for, but readership is intended to be determined by reading attainment, not chronological age.

Do Trackers support the National Literacy Strategy and the National Curriculum in England and Wales?

Yes. Although none of the books is specifically linked to particular reading objectives (in order that they are not seen to be directed at any particular age group) the texts are carefully written to be rich enough in both language and content for age-appropriate discussions and investigations. The Key Stage 2 and 3 objectives in the NLS (National Literacy Strategy) have been borne in mind both in the texts and in the Guided Reading Booklets which accompany each text.

The non-fiction text types chosen for *Trackers* are those specified most commonly in the *NLS Framework* and the topics are all relevant to the National Curriculum and to the QCA programmes of study. Specific cross-curricular links are suggested for each book and pages 19–21 contain suggestions for integrating the books into class topics and projects. Many of these suggestions are consistent with the Literacy Across the Curriculum advice given to Key Stage 3 teachers.

Do Trackers support the Education 5–14 guidelines in Scotland and the National Curriculum in Northern Ireland?

Yes. All the *Trackers* titles have been checked by an expert in Scotland and do support the guidelines, both in literacy and across the wider curriculum. Again, no specific references and objectives are shown, but expected learning outcomes are made explicit.

Do Trackers ***help to accelerate reading ability?***
Yes, in two main ways:

★ *By promoting age-appropriate reading skills*
Children aged 7+ who struggle with reading tend to experience difficulty across the curriculum because information and resources are increasingly delivered through the written word. Many children who find reading hard are otherwise capable of accessing an age-appropriate curriculum and these children need to develop 'book awareness' understanding (e.g. how non-fiction books are organised; how authors create characters and settings) in order that they can track the progress made by their peers.

★ *By challenging children to try to read slightly more complex language*
All ***Trackers*** books have two levels of text: the main text which is very structured (see pages 17 and 18) and additional 'secondary' text which is slightly more challenging. Experience from trialling shows that most of the children who could read the main text in a book were eager to attempt the more challenging secondary text and they were often successful.

What is the difference between 'main text' and 'secondary text'?

Main text: The main text in each book is carefully structured to promote gradual, secure progression through the development of different skills and strategies for reading (see page 14). This text is always clearly marked by some design device that is identified on the inside front cover of each book. If children only read the main text in any book, the book will make complete sense and be a satisfying read.

The main text is intended to be at the child's instructional level (i.e. they can read about 90 – 95% independently and accurately). This is the text children should work at independently in guided reading sessions.

The main text is used to calculate the word count, phonic focus and high frequency words for each book.

Secondary text: In all the books, there is additional text whose purpose varies depending on the text type or genre. The secondary text is usually at the level above the main text, so when the children move to the next level of ***Trackers*** they will be well prepared for its challenges.

This secondary text has three main functions:
★ to offer an additional level of challenge which encourages children to try to stretch their reading abilities within a secure and motivating context;
★ to give additional information which increases the readership of the book and the understanding and enjoyment of each reader;
★ to provide age-appropriate book features which can be mediated by an adult to help to develop the children's age-appropriate reading behaviours and understanding.

In the non-fiction, some features are consistently counted as secondary text in all text types. These include:
★ *all the organisational features of the books* (contents page, index, headings, glossaries, blurb): It is expected that these features will primarily be used in the context of an adult teaching the children to use these features efficiently and correctly to find information. Most of the words used for headings etc. are 'content' words which are easily read in the context of the pictures and the on-going text, but which are not expected to be read in isolation. Since they are read with an adult, glossaries and indexes include words from the secondary text throughout the book.
★ *the 'look back' section:* Most of the non-fiction books include a 'look back' section which encourages children to revisit the book to find specific information. The index is printed on the same double page spread as the 'look back' section in order that the children can be taught to make use of the index to find answers to the questions. Again, it is anticipated that this activity will be mediated by an adult, so the 'look back' section is secondary text.

Scope and sequence charts

Level 1: Elephant tracks – non-fiction

COME CLOSER — Text type: Report

Total number of words: 74 — Number of different words: 45
Total number of sentences: 12 — Average sentence length: 6 words

Trackers high frequency words
and, at, big, but, do, I, in, is ,it, look, me, of, the, this, we, you, your

'Tricky' words
earth, island, solar system, UK, universe, years

Words with consonant blends
across, address, from, let's, planet, space, start

Useful strategies
Splitting words into syllables, e.g. _a-cross, ad-dress, bill-i-ons, plan-et_

OUTSIDE ART — Text type: Report

Total number of words: 104 — Number of different words: 49
Total number of sentences: 13 — Average sentence length: 8 words

Trackers high frequency words
a, all, and, are, in, is, look, make, many, of, out, the, to, you

'Tricky' words
different, does, move, season, water

Words with consonant blends
from, grown, last, places, plant, wind

Useful strategies
Recognition of plural -s endings, e.g. _places, seasons, sorts, plants, shapes, sounds, things_

MEET THE FLEETS — Text type: Puzzle

Total number of words: 190 — Number of different words: 68
Total number of sentences: 25 — Average sentence length: 8 words

Trackers high frequency words
a, and, back, do, in, like, look, name, of, on, that, the, this, to

'Tricky' words
answer, data, Lola, questions, why

Words with consonant blends
and, around, Fleets, grandpa, granny, help, people, questions, rest, sleeps

Useful strategies
Splitting words into syllables, e.g. _Grand-pa, rem-em-ber, fam-i-ly_

HAWK EYES — Text type: Puzzle

Total number of words: 195	Number of different words: 101
Total number of sentences: 23	Average sentence length: 8 words

Trackers high frequency words
a, and, are, at, can, here, I, in, is, it, look, make, many, next, of, on, the, this, three, trees, two, up, we, went, what, will, with, you

'Tricky' words
cream, doors, every, matching, people, reptile, sentence, word

Words with consonant blends
clap, class, cliff, cream, grid, next, people, snakes, stamp, sting, three, tray, tree, umbrella, went

Useful strategies
Recognition of plural -s endings, e.g. animals, balloons, boxes, dogs, doors, letters, nets, rabbits, sentences, trees, umbrellas, words

IT'S MAGIC! — Text type: Instruction

Total number of words: 398	Number of different words: 146
Total number of sentences: 61	Average sentence length: 6 words

Trackers high frequency words
a, and, are, at, back, big, can, do, from, he, here, I, in, is, it, make, many, me, next, no, of, on, one, out, put, that, the, then, this, three, to, two, up, was, what, who, will, with

'Tricky' words
abracadabra, audience, bright, double, finally, friend, 'ladies and gentlemen', modelling, money, right, scissors, through

Words with consonant blends
black, bright, clay, empty, first, from, friend, hand, lift, next, scoop, steps, stick, tray

Useful strategies
Recognising common suffixes, e.g. bigg-er, bigg-est, coin-s, modell-ing

EARTHLING STUDY SKILLS — Text type: Instruction

Total number of words: 358	Number of different words: 146
Total number of sentences: 85	Average sentence length: 4 words

Trackers high frequency words
a, an, are, big, but, can, do, here, I, in, is, it, like, look, me, no, of, one, that, the, this, to, up, we, what, will, you, your

'Tricky' words
any, answer, ask, bright, colours, dining, earth, illustrations, know, listen, other, questions

Words with consonant blends
best, bright, children, clean, clearly, dress, find, first, help, lunch, must, people, please, respect, Spim, think, throw, Trax

Useful strategies
Recognising common suffixes, e.g. teach-er, clear-ly, learn-ing, hand-s

Level 1: Elephant tracks – fiction

THE BIG MESS

Total number of words: 259	Number of different words: 100
Total number of sentences: 51	Average sentence length: 5 words

Trackers high frequency words
a, and, asked, at, back, big, but, can, didn't, he, here, I, in, is ,it, like, look, me, next, no, of, on, out, put, said, that, the, to, up, was, went, will, with

'Tricky' words
classroom, doesn't, don't, lunchtime, Mant, new, school, teacher

Words with consonant blends
Blop, crisp(s), drop, dump, just, last, lunch, Plop, Slig, slot, snack, stop, watch

Useful strategies
Understanding contractions: *didn't, don't, he's, it's, what's*

BUZZ BALL

Total number of words: 253	Number of different words: 89
Total number of sentences: 47	Average sentence length: 5 words

Trackers high frequency words
a, and, asked, but, he, I, in, is, it, like, look, next, no, on, put, said, that, the, this, to, up, was, we, went, what, will, with, you

'Tricky' words
lunchtime, playtime, school, something, why

Words with consonant blends
fast, Glitch, grin, lost, pack, play, stop, strong, switched, switching, twit

Useful strategies
Compound words: *lunch + time, play + time, some + thing*

CATCH IT, TIZZ!

Total number of words: 241	Number of different words: 92
Total number of sentences: 48	Average sentence length: 5 words

Trackers high frequency words
a, and, are, asked, at, back, but, can, didn't, do, he, here, I, in, is, it, like, look, make, next, no, of, on, out, said, that, the, then, this, to, was, we, went

'Tricky' words
lesson, school, switched, teacher, wasn't

Words with consonant blends
best, Blop, catch, clank, crash, fast, Glitch, help, jumped, quick, smash

Useful strategies
Understanding contractions: *can't, didn't, it's, wasn't, where's*

THE DUCK FROM ZOG

Total number of words: 194	Number of different words: 76
Total number of sentences: 32	Average sentence length: 6 words

Trackers high frequency words

a, after, and, asked, at, back, big, but, can, didn't, do, fast, he, here, I, is, it, like, look, no, of, on, one, out, said, the, then, this, to, up, was, we, went

'Tricky' words

come, why

Words with consonant blends

catch, crisp(s), croc, duck, fetch, from, help, jump, last, play, stick, trick(s)

Useful strategies

Recognition of -ed endings: *asked, jumped, looked, picked*

Level 2: Frog tracks – non-fiction

SKELETON CLUES — Text type: Report

Total number of words: 153	Number of different words: 71
Total number of sentences: 16	Average sentence length: 9 words

Trackers high frequency words

a, and, are, at, big, but, can, find, from, have, how, in, is, like, look, of, on, one, out, that, the, these, they, to, use, we, what, which

'Tricky' words

chimpanzee, dinosaur, dolphin, family, human, skeleton, water

Words with consonant blends

and, dry, find, from, land, lots, must, past, skeleton, skull, under

Useful long vowel phonemes

'ue' in *clue, human, to, used* etc.

'ee' in *been, chimpanzee, eat, sea, teeth, these* etc.

Useful strategies

Splitting words into syllables, e.g. *chimp-an-zee, dol-phin*

PICK OUT A PERSON — Text type: Puzzle

Total number of words: 232	Number of different words: 96
Total number of sentences: 14	Average sentence length: 15 words

Trackers high frequency words

a, and, big, can, find, in, is, no, of, on, out, the, what, who, with

'Tricky' words

catching, colour, jacket, photo, satellite, tongue, walking, water, woman

Words with consonant blends

blue, child, driver, flags, flowers, glasses, green, number, people, purple, step, stick, sunglasses, three, train, tray, watch

Useful long vowel phonemes

'or' in *ball, four, more, walking, water* etc.

'ir' in *person, purple, turn, word* etc.

Useful strategies

Making good use of keys and picture cues.

A WEEK WITH THE FLEETS   Text type: Puzzle

| Total number of words: 298 | Number of different words: 147 |
| Total number of sentences: 47 | Average sentence length: 6 words |

Trackers high frequency words
a, are, at, can, do, find, for, go, have, I, in, is, it, like, look, me, of, on, out, that, the, them, there, they, to, up, want, what, when, which, who, with, you, your

'Tricky' words
cheating, computer, front, groups, near, people, together, treasure

Words with consonant blends
and, drinks, first, Fleet, front, golden, granny, help, last, lost, people, plan, platform, play, salt, snails, stand, stuck, train, treasure

Useful long vowel phonemes
'ee' in *being, eat, cheating, Fleets, material, need, please, week* etc.
'ue' in *do, group, lose, new, room, together, too, who* etc.

Useful strategies
Splitting words into syllables, e.g. *cheat-ing, gold-en, hol-i-day*

SAND, KIPPERS OR ALIENS?   Text type: Instruction

| Total number of words: 448 | Number of different words: 171 |
| Total number of sentences: 78 | Average sentence length: 5 words |

Trackers high frequency words
a, and, are, but, can, do, first, for, go, have, here, how, in, is, it, like, look, make, me, next, of, on, one, put, that, the, these, they, this, three, to, two, up, use, we, what's, when, with, you, your

'Tricky' words
alien, bored, coin, finally, finish, half, newspaper, points, ready, steady, scissors, who, whole, why

Words with consonant blends
blow, draw, end, fewest, floor, fold, kind, number, place, player, point, sand, spade, start, steady, stop, swim, throw, tray, try, want

Useful long vowel phonemes
'ai' in *aim, alien, away, later, paper, taking, wait, way* etc.
'ie' in *behind, dice, eye, finally, kind, line, my, try, why* etc.

Useful strategies
Splitting words into syllables, e.g. *news-pap-er, fin-al-ly, kip-per*

EYE TRICKS   Text type: Instruction

| Total number of words: 441 | Number of different words: 159 |
| Total number of sentences: 36 | Average sentence length: 12 words |

Trackers high frequency words
a, and, are, at, big, can, for, from, here, how, in, is, it, look, make, many, of, on, one, that, the, them, then, there, these, they, this, to, two, up, use, what, will, with, you, your

'Tricky' words
beyond, circles, computer, diagonally, further, middle, parallel, picture, scissors, squared

Words with consonant blends
across, ask, bend, blue, brain, close, computer, draw, floating, friend, front, hands, hold, impossible, match, paste, pencil, point, prongs, simple, small, square, trace, trick

Useful long vowel phonemes
'ai' in *away, brain, make, page, paper, paste, same, trace* etc.
'ie' in *eye, like, line, side, sign, time, try, why, wide, write* etc.

Useful strategies
Splitting words into syllables, e.g. *in-struc-tions, par-all-el, pen-cil*

ZERO GRAVITY

Text type: Report

Total number of words: 211	Number of different words: 106
Total number of sentences: 26	Average sentence length: 8 words

Trackers high frequency words

a, and, at, back, can, do, first, go, have, here, in, is, it, like, make, no, of, on, one, them, there, this, three, to, two, up, use, we, when, which, will, you

'Tricky' words

astronaut, blood, discovered, experiments, force, gravity, muscles, Newton, pencil, sickness, suction, toilet, usually, vacuum cleaner

Words with consonant blends

blood, cleaner, experiments, gravity, help, pencil, small, space, soft, stay, strong, strange

Useful long vowel phonemes

'oa' in *almost, astronaut, bones, don't, goes, micro, no, zero* etc.
'ai' in *change, day, makes, space, strange, take, way* etc.

Useful strategies

Splitting words into syllables, e.g. *ex-per-i-ment, grav-i-ty, sick-ness*

Level 2: Frog tracks – fiction

BIG BAD SLIG

Total number of words: 265	Number of different words: 108
Total number of sentences: 37	Average sentence length: 7 words

Trackers high frequency words

a, and, are, asked, at, big, but, can, go(ing), he, how, I, in, it, just, look, make, me, next, of, on, out, put, said, the, them, then, they, this, three, to, up, very, was, we, what, when

'Tricky' words

afraid, cupboard, eight, laughing, machine, shrink

Words with consonant blends

afraid, bent, Blop, class, cross, friends, Glitch, grow, just, little, must, next, plan, shrink, Slig, spider, stuck, test, three

Useful long vowel phonemes

'ow' in *about, how, out* etc.
'ai' in *afraid, came, eight, made, make, they*

Useful strategies

Common word endings: *laugh-ing, friend-s, push-ed*

THE COPY CAT

Total number of words: 332	Number of different words: 108
Total number of sentences: 46	Average sentence length: 7 words

Trackers high frequency words

a, and, back, but, can, didn't, do, for, from, front, he, I, in, is, it, just, look, me, no, of, one, out, said, that, the, them, then, there, they, this, up, was, went, what, when, who, with

'Tricky' words

afraid, classroom, front, person, school, smashed, threw, waited, walked, water

Words with consonant blends

afraid, classroom, children, front, grin, lots, past, school, smashed, told, window

Useful long vowel phonemes

'or' in *all, fall, moral, saw, walked, water* etc.
'ai' in *afraid, made, they, waited* etc.

Useful strategies

Common word endings: *jump-ed, thing-s*

JUST LIKE ON EARTH

Total number of words: 223	Number of different words: 106
Total number of sentences: 37	Average sentence length: 6 words

Trackers high frequency words
a, and, are, at, big, but, can, didn't, do, for, go(ing), he, have, I, in, is, it, just, like, look, next, no, of, on, put, said, that, the, there, they, to, up, very, want, was, we, went, with

'Tricky' words
balloon, Earth, fizzy, friends, parties, pulled

Words with consonant blends
asked, bent, best, Blop, class, drinks, friends, Glitch, held, help, jump, just, landed, lots, people, play, wanted

Useful long vowel phonemes
'oa' in *don't, home, ok, rope* etc.
'ar' in *(asked, class), party, parties* etc.

Useful strategies
Common word endings: *drink-s, part-ies, land-ed*

GETTING ON THE TEAM

Total number of words: 245	Number of different words: 114
Total number of sentences: 34	Average sentence length: 7 words

Trackers high frequency words
a, and, at, but, can, didn't, do, first, for, go(ing), he, I, in, it, just, like, me, next, of, on, out, said, the, then, there, this, to, very, want, was, went, with

'Tricky' words
children, friends, Mr, pitch, school, turn, won't

Words with consonant blends
best, Block, children, crash, dreams, drop, fast, flew, Friday, friends, hands, help, just, last, most, pitch, play, school, Slig, still, stop, test, think, try, watch

Useful long vowel phonemes
'ee' in *be, dreams, he, me, she, team* etc.
'ir' in *earth, first, turn, were* etc.

Useful strategies
Understanding apostrophes for possession: *Slig's, Tizz's;*
and contraction: *it's, there's*

Text types and genres

Trackers includes books from a range of text types and genres because they present different reading challenges and offer opportunities for teaching a variety of reading strategies (including, for instance: a range of purposes for reading, a variety of comprehension strategies and different strategies for decoding print). The language conventions for each different text type also varies, and this is reflected in the overall word count.

Fiction

Trackers level	Number of words	Number of pages	Book titles
1 Elephant tracks	150–220	16	The Big Mess; Buzz Ball; Catch it, Tizz!; The Duck from Zog
2 Frog tracks	250–280	16	Big Bad Slig; The Copy Cat; Just Like On Earth; Getting on the Team

There are four fiction books at each level. The books are science fiction and centre around a group of children at a school on the planet Zap. The 'point of view' character is an Earth boy called Nick and his teachers and classmates are all aliens of one sort or another.

The overall word count of the fiction books is lower than the word count for most of the non-fiction books and there is often less text on each page. This is because of the particular challenges that narrative fiction books present to the reader, including the fact that stories often involve more abstract ideas and that the readers have to sustain their understanding throughout a whole book. The fiction books have been written with these challenges in mind, and the text and pictures work well together to support the reader in understanding the story.

Picture cues can be helpful in fiction books, but children do need to be able to decode a lot of text without them. For this reason, there is a strong emphasis on the use of phonically regular words and high frequency words in these texts. Content words for each book (e.g. *school, class, teacher*) are indicated on the front cover of the Guided Reading Booklets. These words are often predictable by the context.

Non-fiction

The different non-fiction text types each have their own conventions that children need to become familiar with. The main text word count varies from text type to text type according to the demands of the language as well as the complexity of the layouts etc. Although there is a progression in the phonics and the high frequency words used in these books, there are also many more 'content words' which are easily readable or predictable in context. As children read these books, they will develop a wide range of reading strategies which include reading on, predicting a word that makes sense, using analogy with other words on the page, reading the pictures, as well as phonic cues and knowledge of high frequency words.

Text length For some children, the process of decoding the text occupies much of their cognitive ability and they have little spare capacity for understanding and remembering what they have read. Non-fiction books tend to have text in 'bite-sized' chunks that can be read and then re-read for understanding.

Pictures Whilst highly illustrated picture books are often associated with younger children, pictures are accepted as an integral part of non-fiction books. When reading non-fiction, children who rely heavily on pictures as a cueing strategy do not have to feel concerned about peer reaction to the level of illustration in the book.

Reading strategies While developing phonic and word recognition skills continues to be important, for many of our target readership the active promotion of text and sentence level reading strategies can be very beneficial. Through the reading of captions and of shorter texts linked to pictures and diagrams, children can be taught to look at reading skills that focus more on monitoring meaning than on decoding individual words.

Non-fiction: report texts

Trackers level	Number of words	Number of pages	Book titles
1 **Elephant tracks**	75–125	16	*Come Closer* (Earth in space; maps) *Outside Art* (art in the environment)
2 **Frog tracks**	150–250	16	*Skeleton Clues* (What we can learn from bones) *Zero Gravity* (life in space without gravity)

Non-fiction: puzzle texts

Trackers level	Number of words	Number of pages	Book titles
1 **Elephant tracks**	150–200	16	*Meet the Fleets* (deductive skills) *Hawk Eyes* (an 'I-spy' book)
2 **Frog tracks**	225–325	16	*Pick Out a Person* (find a person in a crowd) *A Week With the Fleets* (deductive skills)

There are two report texts at each level of *Trackers* because reports are the most common non-fiction text type that children are likely to meet in school and they need to know how to read them. In these books the main text can be quite short, giving just enough information to create a context so that children can understand and interpret the pictures, diagrams and charts. On the other hand, there are substantial opportunities for adding information through secondary text.

Report texts have the lowest main text word count of the *Trackers* text types. This is due to:
★ the other demands of the text type. Children need to be taught to read and interpret all the information on a spread including how to use the heading, any sub-headings, captions, photographs, illustrations, diagrams, charts, maps, keys, etc. Although the more accessible main text is clearly marked on all spreads, the design of each page is otherwise age-appropriate and includes the full range of features associated with report texts.
★ the increased amount of secondary text. Report texts have more secondary text, adding information, than any of the other text types. This presents an extra level of challenge for children who are gaining in confidence.
The report texts contain interesting new information that will enrich cross-curricular explorations for the whole class.

Interactive puzzle texts are unique to *Trackers*. Visual literacy is developed as children search pictures for clues and interpret them to find answers to the questions. These are immediately very motivating books in which the purpose of reading is apparent – you need to read the text in order to find out what you need to do! Some of the puzzles are very short, with all the information you need on one page; others demand more looking back and forth in the book to confirm and compare pictures and information.

As children read the puzzle books and do the puzzles, they develop many higher order reading skills such as skimming and scanning, searching for patterns and meaning, logical thinking, deduction and inference. They also learn to distinguish between comprehension strategies required to develop understanding over a whole book and those required to understand the text within a sentence.

Main text always gives required information and poses questions. Secondary text can be used to ask additional, more searching questions and is sometimes used to add information that might be necessary to answer other questions in the secondary text.

Non-fiction: instruction/procedural texts

Trackers level	Number of words	Number of pages	Book titles
1 Elephant tracks	350–400	16	*Earthling Study Skills* (how pupils on earth should behave) *It's Magic!* (simple magic tricks)
2 Frog tracks	425–475	16	*Sand, Kippers or Aliens?* (games for a wet playtime) *Eye Tricks* (visual illusions)

Instruction (or procedural) text is a familiar non-fiction text type. The main text in these books is inevitably longer than in report texts, because every step in the instruction has to be in the main text. Secondary text is used for additional comments, safety instructions and advice.

As well as presenting straightforward instruction texts, these books also recognise the way that children meet instructions in their everyday life, for example in dialogue and school rules. All of the instructions in the books are for things that children can do in school using equipment normally found in the classroom.

There are two instruction texts at each of the first two levels of *Trackers*, one at each of the third and fourth levels and thereafter instruction texts are found in some of the 'magazine' format books.

Non-fiction: recount texts

There is one long recount text at each of levels 3 and 4, and thereafter recount texts are in most of the 'magazine' format books.

Trackers includes two kinds of recount text: recounts which are written in the present tense because they relate to day-to-day experiences, and recounts which are written largely in the past tense because they focus mainly on one experience.

Non-fiction: 'magazine' format books

The 'magazine' format books are books that include two or three different text types which are related to a common theme. This format gives children the opportunity to recognise that there is more than one way of presenting information, and of directly comparing the pros and cons of using different types for particular purposes.

Structure

The development of skills through *Trackers* is carefully structured to ensure that children make appropriate progress while existing skills are consolidated and made secure. In order to give opportunities for adequate reinforcement, there are a total of 10 books at each level (four fiction and six non-fiction) and six levels of books to span the reading ages from approximately 5:9 to 7:6.

The level descriptions in the Book Bands reference book (UK Reading Recovery National Network) have been used to give guidance as to text features which are appropriate at each level, but since *Trackers* is aimed at an older target readership, some of the Book Bands level descriptors are inappropriate (for example, we have a greater amount of text on a page; we

have more pages in a book; we have more complex story lines). We have, however, structured the degree of support given to the reader through the development of features such as:

★ consistency of sentence structure and how closely sentence structure reflects spoken language;
★ predictability of story line;
★ relationship between text and pictures;
★ phonic skills necessary to decode phonically regular words;
★ percentage of high frequency, or phonically regular, words.

The following table shows the structured progression within *Trackers* of some of these skills and strategies:

Trackers level	Word count (see also text type descriptions)	Number of pages	Phonic focus	Average sentence length	High frequency words
1 Elephant tracks	75–400	16	Initial and final consonant blends	5–6 words	50
2 Frog tracks	150–475	16	Initial and final consonant blends	6 words	+15
3 Giraffe tracks	300–510	16	Introducing common long vowel phonemes	6–7 words	+20
4 Parrot tracks	500–720	24	Consolidating common long vowel phonemes	6–7 words	+30
5 Tiger tracks	620–920	24	Introducing other long vowel phonemes	7+ words	+50
6 Zebra tracks	690–970	24	Consolidating other long vowel phonemes	7+ words	+50

★ *Word count and number of pages* The rise in word count and page numbers reflects the expectation that reading stamina and proficiency are developing. The variations of word count within a level are appropriate to the different text types.
★ *Phonic focus* This progression of phonic skills is consistent with that recommended in DfES phonics programmes. The 'phonic focus' does not imply that the books exclusively use words with these letter patterns, but that there is a preponderance of such words where possible. This is particularly apparent in the fiction books.

★ *Average sentence length* There is no direct correlation between the difficulty of a text and sentence length, but average sentence length can be an indication of the increasing difficulty of texts. Sometimes, longer sentences are easier to read because they can clarify the relationship between two otherwise unconnected sentences.
★ *High frequency words* These are words which are used frequently across all the books in a level. The *Trackers* high frequency words for levels 1 and 2 are listed in the table on page 18.

Trackers level	Cumulative high frequency (H/F) words*
1 **Elephant tracks**	a, and, are, asked, at, back, big, but, can, do, didn't, from, he, here, I, in, is, it, like, look, make, many, me, name, next, no, of, on, one, out, put, said, that, the, then, this, three, to, two, up, use, was, we, went, what, who, with, will, you, your
2 **Frog tracks**	find, first, for, go, have, how, just, them, there, these, they, very, when, which

* High frequency words are cumulative (i.e. words introduced at one level will continue to be reinforced at the next) and are found in several books at the level. They are largely consistent with words recommended in most high frequency word lists.

Other, less measurable, ways in which *Trackers* books are structured are:

★ *Content* The earlier books, both fiction and non-fiction, have cognitively less demanding content than the later books. As the children read through the levels they will encounter increasingly demanding ideas.

★ *'Word attack' strategies* In the Guided Reading Booklets for the first levels, fairly simple strategies are suggested which build on familiar strategies children have been developing since they began reading (e.g. sounding out and sounding out by syllable). During level 3, more 'meaning based' strategies are introduced and children are also asked to segment or 'chunk' words into familiar letter patterns as they meet more long vowel phonemes.

★ *Page design* Although designers always design books individually, there are fewer constraints in the higher levels. This means, for example, that there are some pages that have a lot more text on them than others. This is consistent with other age-appropriate books children will meet in the classroom. The text will, of course, still be very structured, but the books will increasingly look like other books.

★ *Comprehension focus* Different kinds of comprehension are the focus of different questions posed in the Guided Reading Booklets. 'Retrieval of detail' questions are suggested to help children to focus on what they have actually read in the book; 'simple inference' questions encourage children to reflect on what they have read and to draw their own conclusions; and 'personal response' questions ask children to give their opinions and to relate what they have read to their own experiences. As children progress through *Trackers*, more searching questions are suggested that require children to use more inferential and deductive comprehension. These require a greater understanding of the text and challenge children to think harder about what they have read.

Literacy across the curriculum

Many children who find reading challenging, or who lack confidence in reading, experience independent research as a daunting task, particularly if they have previously been encouraged to engage only at a literal level with text (for example, simply locating information rather than truly understanding it). Finding information independently, however, is a skill that all children need to develop. Non-fiction *Trackers* can help to achieve this in a number of ways.

Teaching information retrieval skills

Although the texts are accessible, the variety of layouts used in *Trackers* is similar to those used in other non-fiction books. You can use these books to teach age-appropriate information retrieval skills in a range of different text types. Use the non-fiction organisational features to teach children to locate information more efficiently. Features included are:

★ covers, title and blurb;
★ contents;
★ index;
★ glossary;
★ main text;
★ headings and sub-headings;
★ captions and labels.

The charts on pages 20 and 21 indicate how the *Trackers* books can be used to support other curriculum areas. *Trackers* have not been written to conform with any particular syllabus, since the emphasis is on the motivational nature of the content and the suitability of the books for different age groups, but many of the books can be linked with cross-curricular work. Since the ideas and information in the *Trackers* books are unlikely to be duplicated by more conventional topic-based library books, the children finding information in *Trackers* will have a unique contribution to make.

Ways of using *Trackers* to support cross-curricular group work in a mixed ability class include the following:

Jigsaw approach

★ Agree on a number of related 'research topics' that children could investigate. Choose a *Trackers* book that will address one of the research topics.
★ Organise the children into mixed ability groups – 'home groups'. Give each child in each group a number (e.g. from 1–6). Ensure that all the children who will be working with *Trackers* have the same number.
★ Call all the number 1s from each of the 'home groups' to work together in an 'expert group', giving them a topic to research and suggesting which classroom resources they might use. This is a collaborative research activity, in which all members of the group must make sure that all other members know the same information that they do.
★ Do the same with each of the other numbered groups, giving *Trackers* to the focus expert group. Make sure they understand what their research topic is.
★ Once all the children have had sufficient time to work, ask them to return to their original 'home group' and ask each member of the group to report what has been found out in the working group. Emphasise the fact that each member of the 'home group' has had access to different information – they must listen to each other in order that they all know what the others have found out. The children who have been reading the *Trackers* book will have to be prepared to communicate their information too.
★ Ask each 'home group' to prepare a presentation to show the rest of the class (or another audience) what they have found out.

Pairs to fours

Pupils work together in pairs. Each pair then joins with another pair to explain and compare ideas. Children who use *Trackers* should be paired together, but can join with a pair using other resources to share their ideas.

Snowball

An extension of the 'pairs to fours' idea. The fours move into groups of eight in order to compare ideas and to sort out the next course of action. Finally the whole class is drawn together and a spokesperson for each group of eight feeds back the group's ideas.

Quiz master

Let groups of children prepare quizzes for other groups. Children reading *Trackers* will have access to information that other children are less likely to find in their books.

Envoys

Once a group has completed an information retrieval task, one member of the group is sent to every other group to explain and summarise what has been found out. The original group then reconvenes to discuss how other groups reacted and to feed back any new information given. For this activity, keep a *Trackers* group working together to find their information. They can then send envoys to other groups and reconsider all the information gained.

Listening triads

Pupils work in groups of three. Each pupil takes the role of talker, questioner or recorder. The talker gives information, the questioner prompts and seeks clarification, and the recorder makes notes and reports back at the end of the conversation. Next time roles are changed. Children who have shared a *Trackers* book can work together in a group of three.

Cross-curricular links with *Trackers* levels 1 and 2

Elephant tracks	Come Closer	Outside Art	Meet the Fleets	Hawk Eyes	It's Magic!	Earthling Study Skills
Maths	Ratios and proportion; scale work		Presenting data; scales	Co-ordinates; counting and estimating; shape	Measuring: doubling	
Science	Earth and beyond	Light and shadow; materials			Light and shadow	
ICT	*Graphic models*		Simulated worlds; spreadsheets			
Geography	Different maps; using secondary evidence	Humans effects on environment; *weather*		Different human environments; using secondary evidence		
History						
Art / Design and technology		Natural art; art and artists		Pattern and viewpoint	Construction following instructions	*'Origami'*
RE / PSHCE*			Family relationships			Respect and consideration
Thinking skills		*Philosophical enquiry*	Deductive thinking	Logical and deductive reasoning		

Italics indicates only a passing reference.
* Personal, Social, Health and Citizenship Education

Frog tracks	Skeleton Clues	Pick Out a Person	A Week With the Fleets	Sand, Kippers or Aliens?	Eye Tricks	Zero Gravity
Maths	*Scale*	Counting and estimating; classification; co-ordinates; data handling	*Sequencing*	Data handling; symmetry	*Shape and space*	
Science	Classification; adaptation; life processes; habitats			Materials; forces	How we see things	Scientific enquiry; forces; life processes
ICT	Recording information		Graphic choices; simulated worlds		*Graphics; modelling effects; identifying patterns; exploring relationships*	
Geography	Patterns and processes; *rivers and mountains*	Different human environments and cultures	Reading different maps; physical characteristics of a place			Earth and beyond
History	Historical interpretation; *archaeology*	Change over time; using secondary evidence; *VE day*				*Apollo flights*
Art / Design and technology				Construction	Starting points for art; tools and materials; *pattern*	*Problem solving*
RE / PSHCE*			Group and family dynamics; *co-operation*	Using rules		
Thinking skills		Logical and deductive reasoning	Logical and deductive reasoning	Strategic thinking	*Philosophical enquiry*	*Reasoning*

Italics indicates only a passing reference.
* Personal, Social, Health and Citizenship Education

Speaking and listening

Some of the children who struggle with reading, particularly those for whom English is an additional or foreign language, are likely to find speaking and listening challenging. This is often because they feel inadequate when faced by their more articulate peers and they don't think that they have a valid contribution to make to a discussion. Encouraging such children to develop their speaking and listening skills is crucial both for their self-esteem and to promote their own intellectual development.

Trackers supports speaking and listening development in a number of key ways:

★ *through group work: Trackers* books can be used in all of the cross-curricular information retrieval ideas suggested above. All these activities involve children in talking and listening, remembering and summarising specific information. This is less threatening than having to form and offer opinions on the spot.

★ *through the exciting content and design: Trackers* books are designed to be poured over and discussed by pairs of children. The 'social' aspect of reading is part of the rationale for the design and format of the non-fiction books in particular.

★ *through the Guided Reading Booklets:* Each *Trackers* book has a Guided Reading Booklet (see page 23) to accompany it which is full of opportunities to develop ideas and concepts through speaking and listening.

★ *through the photocopiable 'leaflet' on pages 94 and 95 of this Guide:* This gives suggestions for guided reading and about asking and answering questions.

Reading and writing

Many children who experience difficulties with reading also find writing challenging. Although *Trackers* is primarily a reading resource, it also promotes writing development:

★ *by providing good models of texts:* children find it difficult to write different kinds of texts if they are not familiar with the basic conventions and language use of the text type. By providing a wide range of well written texts – albeit using comparatively simple language structures – *Trackers* offers good models on which children can base their own writing.

★ *by scaffolding information gathering techniques:* for each non-fiction *Trackers* book there is a photocopy master (PCM) worksheet which presents a framework for children to find and record information. This activity has a dual purpose: it promotes reading for meaning and information sorting strategies whilst at the same time offering a model for ways in which information can be gathered and recorded as a preparation for writing.

Using *Trackers* in the classroom

Trackers books are intended to be used for three purposes:
1. for children to browse through, enjoy and share with their friends and family;
2. to support cross-curricular classroom projects, as described on pages 19–21;
3. for guided reading, supported by either a teacher or a teaching assistant.

Using *Trackers* for guided reading

To support you in using *Trackers* for guided reading, each *Trackers* book is accompanied by:
★ pages in this Teacher's Guide that give you information about each book including the blurb, lists of high frequency and 'tricky' words, the phonic focus, useful decoding strategies, suggested cross-curricular links and information about the photocopy master (PCM) worksheets;
★ three PCMs for each non-fiction book and two for each fiction book. For all the books, the first PCM addresses word level skills that help to develop reading fluency and accuracy, and the second PCM focuses on reading comprehension. The third non-fiction PCM always scaffolds a writing task based on the book;
★ a Guided Reading Booklet.

Guided Reading Booklet

The Guided Reading Booklet can be used by teaching assistants or parent helpers working with a group. It includes a format for organising guided reading sessions and suggests ways to introduce each book so that the children are more likely to achieve success. There are also discussion points for a final session in which the children consider what they have achieved. For the fiction books, this final section includes comprehension questions that develop SATs-type comprehension skills, focusing on 'retrieval of detail', 'simple inference' and 'personal response'.

In addition, the Guided Reading Booklet gives page by page suggestions, including:
★ discussion points to make sure that the children are understanding the progression of the text;
★ information about layout. This is particularly

useful for the non-fiction books since part of the skill of information retrieval in non-fiction is understanding how the information is presented;
★ ways of introducing and exploring 'tricky' words that are appropriate to the reading strategies being developed.

For each double page spread there is a 'follow on' box. This contains word and sentence level features (e.g. punctuation, style, word choice, fonts used) which children need to understand. It also contains a 'making meaning' feature which encourages children to think around the text on the page, making links to their own experiences or general knowledge and developing inferential comprehension.

Leaflet

More general information about organising guided reading sessions is given in the A5 photocopiable leaflet on pages 94 and 95 of this Guide. This leaflet is written for teaching assistants and parent helpers, and suggests ways of organising a series of sessions around a book. It also explains how asking as well as answering questions can help to develop a child's understanding of a book and motivate them to read.

Home/school links using *Trackers*

Children will enjoy reading *Trackers* so much that they will be keen to take them home to re-read with parents and carers. Depending on your school policy, you may be happy to send the books home, or you may prefer to keep sets intact in school. Either way, the worksheets for each book can make good homework activities. For this reason, at least one of the worksheets for each book can be completed without direct reference to the *Trackers* book (although children will need to have read the *Trackers* book in order to understand the activity).

If your school policy is to keep sets of books in school, the suggested cross-curricular ideas in the teaching notes of this Guide (e.g. page 26) could be useful for homework activities.

If you do send books home, the photocopiable

If you do send books home, the photocopiable sheet on page 25 'Reading *Trackers* books together at home' may help parents to continue the school's good practice in developing each child's reading.

Which level of *Trackers* should a child be reading?

As you become more familiar with **Trackers**, you will gain a better understanding of how it fits with other reading resources you use, and which children will read most happily at which levels.

The following chart may be helpful:

Trackers level	Associated Book Band level (see page 17)	Approximate National Curriculum level	Scottish 5–14 level	NI Curriculum level
1 Elephant tracks	Blue	Working within level 1	Working within level A	Working towards level 2
2 Frog tracks	Green	Working within level 1	Working within level A	Working towards level 2
3 Giraffe tracks	Orange	Working towards level 2	Working towards level B	Working within level 2
4 Parrot tracks	Turquoise	Working towards level 2	Working towards level B	Working within level 2
5 Tiger tracks	Purple	Working within level 2	Working within level B	Working within level 2
6 Zebra tracks	Gold	Working within level 2	Working within level B	Working within level 2

For ease of use in the classroom, note that *Trackers* levels are organised alphabetically. When a child is ready to move on, you don't have to look up the next level – just go to the next one in alphabetical order.

Using the *Trackers* reading profile

Photocopy page 96 and use it as you do a detailed assessment of children's reading skills and strategies and their knowledge about reading. The *Elephant tracks* statements summarise the skills needed to read the *Elephant tracks* books, the *Frog tracks* statements summarise the skills needed to read the *Frog tracks* books. The statements at each level are not mutually exclusive and it is unlikely that any one of the profiles will exactly match each child. You can use the profile to do a 'best fit' assessment to make initial decisions before trying out *Trackers* at that level.

★ If a child cannot read unknown consonant-vowel-consonant (CVC) words (e.g. *cat*),

recognises fewer than 50 high frequency words (see page 18 for the **Trackers** 50 high frequency words) and can't track a text from left to right across a page, then **Trackers** is probably too challenging;

★ If you can tick some, but not all of the *Elephant tracks* statements, then the child is probably ready to read *Elephant tracks*;

★ If you can tick all the *Elephant tracks* and some of the *Frog tracks* statements, then the child is probably ready to begin reading *Frog tracks*;

★ If you can tick all the *Elephant tracks* and all the *Frog tracks* statements, then the child may be ready to begin reading *Giraffe tracks*. (See *Teacher's Guide 2* for the reading profile for *Giraffe tracks* and *Parrot tracks*.)

Reading *Trackers* books together at home

Reading *Trackers* fiction books

- Look at the covers, title and blurb. Talk about what you think the book might be about.
- 'Talk the book' together. This involves leafing through the book and:
  - talking about what is happening so that your child gets a good idea of what the story line is;
  - pointing out, for example, names, repeated words and phrases, words you think may be hard to read.

  This activity should only last for two or three minutes, but it will give your child more confidence and understanding.
- Let your child read the book to you. If s/he gets stuck on a word, you can help by:
  - talking about the sounds in the word, if it is easy to sound out;
  - re-reading from the beginning of the sentence;
  - pointing to a picture cue;
  - pointing to a similar word s/he has already read;
  - reading out the word, then asking her/him to re-read the sentence;
  - praising all reasonable attempts.
- Talk about the book again.
- Thank and congratulate your child for sharing the book with you.

Reading *Trackers* non-fiction books

- Use the cover, title and blurb to discuss what you think the book is going to be about.
- Leaf through the book together, looking at the contents page, the headings, the pictures etc. and list some things you might be going to discover in the book. Can your child suggest any questions the book might answer?
- Look through the contents and then the book again, trying to work out its 'shape'. Consider why the author chose to organise the information as she has done. Knowing this information before you read a book is helpful when you're trying to understand what the book is about.
- Let your child read the book – or sections of the book – to you. Use the ideas above to help with any 'tricky' words.
- Talk about what you found out and discuss whether your earlier questions were answered. If not, can your child suggest how s/he might find out answers to the questions? (A different book? Internet?)
- Thank and congratulate your child for sharing the book with you.

Come Closer

Author: Sarah Fleming
Genre: non-fiction   **Text type:** report
Pictures: mostly photographic; some computer graphics

Sam writes his complete address, including continent, planet, solar system. The book examines each line of his address in turn, giving information on size, illustrations/photographs and other details.

Main information about the book

Total number of words: 74   Number of different words: 45
Total number of sentences: 12   Average sentence length: 6 words

---

Trackers high frequency words
and, at, big, but, do, I, in, is, it, look, me, of, the, this, we, you, your

---

'Tricky' words
earth, island, solar system, UK, universe, years

Words with consonant blends
across, address, from, let's, planet, space, start

Useful strategies
Splitting words into syllables, e.g. *a-cross, ad-dress, bill-i-ons, plan-et*

Cross-curricular links

Geography
★ Use appropriate vocabulary to describe geographical features.
★ Use maps and plans at a range of scales.
★ Use secondary sources of information, including aerial photographs.
★ Use as the basis for own work on investigating the locality.

Science
★ Link to projects exploring The Earth and Beyond.

Maths
★ Use scale work to introduce simple ratios and proportions.

Linked PCMs

***Word level work** (p.27) finding words within words*
★ Practise finding 'hidden' words using words on the cover.

★ Talk about how hidden words are sometimes pronounced the same as they are in the longer word (as in *close–closer*) but they are sometimes pronounced differently (as in *lose–close*).

***Reading for meaning** (p.28) sequencing information*
★ Look again at the headings in the book and make sure that the children can read all the words now.
★ Ask the children if they know their own address. Can they spell all the relevant words?
★ They can refer to the book as they do the activity.

***Writing** (p.29) labelling a diagram and writing simple sentences*
★ Reread the main text on page 4.
★ Can the children say a sentence about each of the planets? Make sure they only say one sentence.
★ Help the children to pronounce the names of each planet. Discuss reading strategies used.

Word hunt

Sometimes you can find hidden words in longer words. This can help you to read the longer word.

Which words can you find in these longer words?

longer word	hidden word
address	dress
start	
universe	
billions	
years	
system	
Earth	
planet	
space	
mountain	

Do you think that finding hidden words can help you to remember how to spell the longer words too?

Address check

Read all the different parts of the address.
Can you put them in order, starting with the smallest?
(Cut them out, or write numbers in the boxes.)

Solar System	☐	Sam Slade	☐
Planet Earth	☐	Oxford	☐
3, Tree Street	☐	Universe	☐
UK	☐		

Use the book to check that you got it right!

Now write your own address.
How much information can you give?

_____

_____

_____

_____

_____

_____

Focus: sequencing information

Do you know the planets?

Which planet is which?
Can you label them?

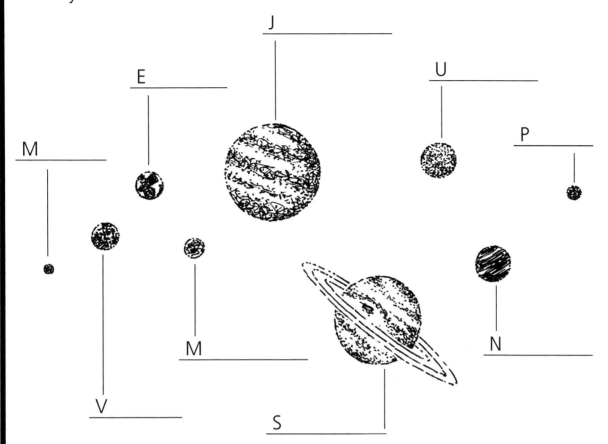

Use pages 4–5 of *Come Closer* to check your answers.

Choose 4 planets and write a sentence about each of them.

1 Earth is the third planet from the sun.

2 _____

3 _____

4 _____

Outside Art

> **Author:** Sarah Fleming
> **Genre:** non-fiction   **Text type:** report
> **Pictures:** photographic

There is more to art than painting and drawing. This book looks at how art can be used to make outside spaces more interesting.

Main information about the book

Total number of words: 104	Number of different words: 49
Total number of sentences: 13	Average sentence length: 8 words

***Trackers* high frequency words**
a, all, and, are, in, is, look, make, many, of, out, the, to, you

'Tricky' words
different, does, move, season, water

Words with consonant blends
from, grown, last, places, plant, wind

Useful strategies
Recognition of plural -s ending, e.g. *places, seasons, sorts, plants, shapes, sounds, things*

Cross-curricular links

Art
* ★ Let children use images and ideas from the book as starting points for their own outside art.
* ★ Discussion arising from the book can help children to appreciate how art can be used to communicate feelings and ideas.
* ★ Children can evaluate the impact on the environment of the outside art in this book and use it to inform their own ideas.
* ★ Discussion about artists and their role as well as a consideration of the materials and processes available are stimulated by the book.

Science
Scientific enquiry – investigative skills:
* ★ physical process: light and shadow;
* ★ materials and their properties: changing materials.

Geography
Link to work on knowledge and understanding of:
* ★ patterns and processes; recognising and explaining patterns made by physical and human features in the environment;
* ★ environmental change; recognising how people can improve or damage the environment.

Linked PCMs

Word level work: (p.31) plural word endings
* ★ Are children familiar with the word 'plural'? Ensure that they understand it means 'more than one'.
* ★ Once children have written the plural forms each time, talk about the word ending 's' used to signify plurals.
* ★ On which page can the children find each of the images?
* ★ The words on pages 4 and 5 are: *places, parks, gardens, woods, fields, streets, squares, grounds.*

Reading for meaning: (p.32) understanding of elements that affect Outside Art
* ★ Ask children to decide what they think the answer is each time, before they check in the book.
* ★ Ask them to consider how each of these elements makes the art more interesting.

Writing: (p.33) using information in the book to contribute to a report text
* ★ Before children write, ask them to rehearse aloud the words they plan to use. In this way, they can concentrate separately on the content while they are speaking, then on spelling and handwriting when they are writing.

More than one

Find pictures like these in the book.
Label them.

| | Which page is the picture on? |

One cow   Three _____   _____

One parrot   Two _____   _____

One head   Lots of _____   _____

One gnome   Lots of _____   _____

Look at pages 4 and 5.
Can you find 8 words that mean 'more than one' of something?
Write them here:

_____   _____   _____   _____

_____   _____   _____   _____

What makes it work?

Do you think each of these kinds of Outside Art is using light, wind or water?

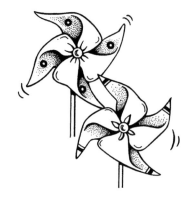

_____

_____

_____

_____

_____

_____

Draw your favourite piece of Outside Art. Why do you like it?

Focus: understanding of elements that affect Outside Art

Writing about Outside Art

Find information in the book to finish the sentences.

Outside Art

Look at pages 4 and 5

You can find Outside Art in

_____

_____

Look at page 6

_____

_____

make being inside different from being outside.

Look at pages 12 and 13

Outside Art does not last as long as inside art because

_____

_____

_____

Meet the Fleets

Author: Sarah Fleming
Genre: non-fiction   **Text type:** puzzle
Pictures: computer graphics

Meet the Fleet Family. Learn about all seven members of the family as you work out who sleeps in which bedroom.

Main information about the book

Total number of words: 190   Number of different words: 68
Total number of sentences: 25   Average sentence length: 8 words

---

Trackers high frequency words
a, and, back, do, in, like, look, name, of, on, that, the, this, to

---

'Tricky' words
answer, data, Lola, questions, why

Words with consonant blends
and, around, Fleets, grandpa, granny, help, people, questions, rest, sleeps

---

Useful strategies
Splitting words into syllables, e.g. *Grand-pa, rem-em-ber, fam-i-ly*

Cross-curricular links

ICT

★ Simulations and models: children can reflect on why computer simulation is used to create 'worlds'. What are the advantages and disadvantages of this medium?

★ Are children familiar with any other simulation programs, either on PCs or on computer games consoles?

★ Use the data on pages 2 and 3 to construct spreadsheets about the Fleet family.

Maths

★ Make links between the presentation of the data on pages 2 and 3 and other kinds of data presentation the children are more familiar with.

★ Discuss the notion of grading on arbitrary scales.

PSHCE

★ Use comments in speech bubbles to explore family dynamics and relationships.

Linked PCMs

Word level work: (p.35) recognising plural suffix 's'
★ Ask children to identify the pictures each time. Can they tell you what each shows? Let them use the page references to confirm.

★ Do children know what the word 'plural' means?

★ Encourage the children to check their spelling each time. All the words are printed, either in the text or as part of the illustration.

★ Talk about plurals such as 'clothes', 'headphones', 'trousers' and 'scissors'. How do we establish one of these?

Reading for meaning: (p.36) using charts to record information
★ This worksheet offers one approach to recording information in order to solve the puzzles in the book. Point out that the lists on the worksheet can be used to sort out the people by recording evidence of their hobbies.

★ After the children have completed the activity, ask them which other information it would have been possible to record in a chart of this kind.

Writing: (p.37) recording data using the book as a model
★ Children should fill in one of the data collection forms to describe themselves and fill in the other for a friend.

★ When they do the drawing activity, remind them of the need to show their interests in the picture.

Give them a name

Label these items from the book.

Look carefully at the end of the word each time.

(pages 4 and 5)

_____

(pages 6 and 7)

_____

(pages 8 and 9)

_____

(pages 12 and 13)

_____

(pages 10 and 11)

_____

(pages 8 and 9)

_____

Focus: recognising plural suffix 's'

Who sleeps where?

Look at the pictures in the book. Tick the boxes to show what there is in each room.
Use the data to find out who sleeps in which room.

This will help you to answer the questions in the book.

BEDROOM A

		Yes	No
	Reading	☐	☐
	Football	☐	☐
	TV	☐	☐
	Snail tank	☐	☐
	Music	☐	☐
	Fitness	☐	☐

Who sleeps here?

_____

BEDROOM B

		Yes	No
	Reading	☐	☐
	Football	☐	☐
	TV	☐	☐
	Painting	☐	☐
	Music	☐	☐
	Computer games	☐	☐

Who sleeps here?

_____

BEDROOM C

		Yes	No
	Reading	☐	☐
	Football	☐	☐
	Models	☐	☐
	Painting	☐	☐
	Snail tank	☐	☐
	TV	☐	☐

Who sleeps here?

_____

BEDROOM D

		Yes	No
	Reading	☐	☐
	Football	☐	☐
	Trumpet	☐	☐
	Painting	☐	☐
	Snail tank	☐	☐
	Computer games	☐	☐

Who sleeps here?

_____

So, who sleeps in Bedroom E? _____

Focus: using charts to record information

What are you like?

Fill in data for you and a friend.

Look at pages 2 and 3 in the book. You could draw a picture too.

Name

Age

Nice

Tidy

Fun

Fit

Hobbies

Job Wanted

Name

Age

Nice

Tidy

Fun

Fit

Hobbies

Job Wanted

Finish drawing this room which you could share with your friend. Think about what should be in it – what pictures, games, etc.

Hawk Eyes

Author: Sarah Fleming
Genre: non-fiction   **Text type:** puzzle
Pictures: photographic

Do you have Hawk Eyes? Can you find little pictures in a bigger picture? Can you look carefully to find answers?

Main information about the book

Total number of words: 195	Number of different words: 101
Total number of sentences: 23	Average sentence length: 8 words

Trackers high frequency words
a, and, are, at, can, here, I, in, is, it, look, make, many, next, of, on, the, this, three, trees, two, up, we, went, what, will, with, you

'Tricky' words
cream, doors, every, matching, people, reptile, sentence, word

Words with consonant blends
clap, class, cliff, cream, grid, next, people, snakes, stamp, sting, three, tray, tree, umbrella, went

Useful strategies
Recognition of plural -s endings, e.g. *animals, balloons, boxes, dogs, doors, letters, nets, rabbits, sentences, trees, umbrellas, words*

Cross-curricular links

Maths

★ Co-ordinates. Use the grids on pages 10 and 11 to talk about co-ordinates.
★ Counting and estimating – counting objects and estimating numbers to 20.
★ Shape. Use the picture on page 3 to talk about 2D and 3D shapes.

Geography

★ Use the photographs on pages 8 and 9 to stimulate geographical discussions about landscapes, land use, environments, where places are.
★ Help children to recognise that using secondary evidence like photographs is a valid geographical tool to raise and discuss issues.

Art/Design and technology

★ Investigate the works of Escher, beginning with the pictures on pages 2 and 3.

Linked PCMs

Word level work: (p.39) segmenting words into syllables
★ Check that children can hear syllables in a word (make a link to the musical rhythm of the word). Do they recognise what a syllable looks like on the page? A working definition is that a syllable contains a vowel and, sometimes, some of the consonants around it.
★ Read the words on the sheet together and agree how many syllables there are in each word.
★ Once the children have completed the activity, ask them to consider how knowing about syllables can help with spelling. There is usually only one syllable in a word that children may have difficulty in spelling. Which is it in these words?

Reading for meaning: (p.40) using the model in the book to write questions about a picture
★ Can the children find the picture in the book that this activity is based on?
★ Talk about the layout and kinds of question the book asks.
★ Ask children to say what they are going to write before they write it.

Writing: (p.41) writing instructions to solve a puzzle
★ Can the children find the picture in the book that this activity is based on?
★ Before they begin to write the instructions, ask them to say aloud what they plan to write.

Tricky words

Find these tricky words in the book.
Show how they can be made into syllables.

The first one has been done for you.

picture

pic	ture

Which is the tricky syllable each time? Colour it in.

sentence

letters

syllable

Draw boxes and write syllables in them for these words:

animals

people

balloons

You ask the questions

Look at this picture of a funfair.
Write some questions like the ones on pages 4 and 5 of the book.

List things for your reader to find.

Think of other questions about the picture to ask your reader. Write them here.

Find:

☺ _____

_____

☺ _____

_____

☺ _____

_____

Other questions:

☺ _____

_____

☺ _____

_____

☺ _____

_____

Focus: using the model in the book to write questions about a picture

Make a puzzle

Make your own puzzle like the one on pages 10 and 11.

Draw your picture on this grid.   Write letters on this grid.

Write the instructions for solving the puzzle here.

_____

_____

_____

_____

_____

_____

Have you told your reader everything they need to know?

Have you told them how to use the picture grid and the letter grid?

Have you drawn the picture squares they need to look at?

Have you given them a hint so they can work out the word?

It's Magic!

Author: Sarah Fleming
Genre: non-fiction   **Text type:** instruction (procedural) text
Pictures: photographs and illustrations

Can you do magic tricks? Follow the instructions in this book, and you will be able to!

Main information about the book

Total number of words: 398   Number of different words: 146
Total number of sentences: 61   Average sentence length: 6 words

Trackers high frequency words
a, and, are, at, back, big, can, do, from, he, here, I, in, is, it, make, many, me, next, no, of, on, one, out, put, that, the, then, this, three, to, two, up, was, what, who, will, with

'Tricky' words
abracadabra, audience, bright, double, finally, friend, 'ladies and gentlemen', modelling, money, right, scissors, through

Words with consonant blends
black, bright, clay, empty, first, friend, from, hand, lift, next, scoop, steps, stick, tray

Useful strategies
Recognising common suffixes, e.g. *bigg-er, bigg-est, coin-s, modell-ing*

Cross-curricular links

Maths
★ Measuring – how will you decide how big to make each of the tubes for the Magic Tubes trick?
★ Doubling and halving – make a chart to show how many coins the magician would have to produce if his friend produced 1, 2, 3, 4, 5 etc. coins.

Science
★ Shadows – explore which coloured card can be used most effectively for the big tube and the secret tube.

Design and technology
★ Cutting – how can the holes in the big tube be cut most effectively and efficiently?
★ Strength – which thickness of card is most appropriate for making the tubes?
★ Modelling clay – determine the characteristics necessary for the modelling clay and design an experiment to test for the most suitable.

Linked PCMs

Word level work: (p.43) recognising common word endings
★ Read the word endings in the sweet jar. What words end with each of these endings?
★ Encourage the children to use the pages given to find the words with their endings.
★ Can the children think of any other endings which could be added to each of these words?

Reading for meaning: (p.44) sequencing visual instructions
★ Can the children use the pictures to sequence the trick? This sequence is based on pages 14–15, as well as pages 8–13.
★ Once they have agreed on the order, ask them to say aloud the instructions for each picture.

Writing: (p.45) sequencing written instructions
★ The children should first read the instructions and decide which order they should appear in.
★ Discuss the kinds of sequencing words that might precede each one – either ordinal words: *first, second, third* etc. or sequencing words like: *first, then, next, after that, finally* etc.
★ The children could combine the instructions and pictures on PCM 2 to make their own book.

Make new words

Write new words by adding an ending to each word.

Find the words in the book to check your spelling.

Use these endings:

big _____ _____
(page 3)

er   s   ly   ing   est

coin _____
(page 9)

final _____
(page 4)

prepare _____
(page 2)

    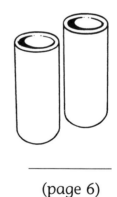

do _____
(page 4)

tube _____
(page 6)

Which of these word endings can you find on page 14?

Write the words:

_____   _____

_____   _____

Focus: recognising common word endings   43

'Double your money' – in pictures

Cut out the pictures and put them in order to show how the
'Double your money' trick is done.
Write the number of the picture in the corner.

Use worksheet PCM 3 to help
you say the instructions.

Focus: sequencing visual instructions

'Double your money' – in words

Cut out the instructions for the 'Double your money' trick and sort them into the right order. Put a word at the beginning of each instruction to help the reader know which order to do the trick in.

_____, put modelling clay under the edge of a table. Stick two coins into the modelling clay.	_____, tell your audience that you will double their money.
_____, work out the trick with a friend.	_____, when you sweep up your friend's coins, scoop up the other two with your left hand.
_____, show the four coins to the audience.	_____, choose your friend to come out from the audience.

Use the pictures on the worksheet PCM 2 and these instructions to make your own book about doing the 'Double your money' trick.

Earthling Study Skills

> **Author:** Sarah Fleming
> **Genre:** non-fiction   **Text type:** instruction (procedural) text
> **Pictures:** illustrations and photographs

Some aliens are coming to Earth. Can they learn how to behave in an Earth classroom?

Main information about the book

Total number of words: 358	Number of different words: 146
Total number of sentences: 85	Average sentence length: 4 words

Trackers high frequency words
a, an, are, big, but, can, do, here, I, in, is, it, like, look, me, no, of, one, that, the, this, to, up, we, what, will, you, your

'Tricky' words
any, answer, ask, bright, colours, dining, earth, illustrations, know, listen, other, questions

Words with consonant blends
best, bright, children, clean, clearly, dress, find, first, help, lunch, must, people, please, respect, Spim, think, throw, Trax

Useful strategies
Recognising common suffixes, e.g. *teach-er, clear-ly, learn-ing, hand-s*

Cross-curricular links

PSHCE
Link to work on:
* rights and responsibilities;
* respect for each other;
* respect for yourself;
* co-operation;
* the need for rules to regulate behaviour in a community.

Linked PCMs

Word level work: (p.47) understanding contractions
* Ask children to read aloud the words in each speech bubble. Can they tell you which two words have been joined together to make the word shown each time?
* Do they recognise that the apostrophe is indicating that letters have been omitted? Can they identify the missing letters each time?
* Once children have completed the first activity, they should try to work out the contracted forms for the second.
* All these words are somewhere in the text. Can the children find them?

Reading for meaning: (p.48) reading definitions and recognising high frequency words
* Check that the children know the conventions of crosswords, including that words can be written from left to right or from top to bottom, and the conventions of numbering crosswords.
* As they read each definition, ask them to check with the word list at the bottom to find the answer.
* Can they find all these words in the book?

Writing: (p.49) writing a book of school rules
* The sheet contains instructions for children to follow to make a little origami-type book.
* Once they have made the book, ask them to think about their book, e.g. how do they plan to use the covers; do they intend to include a contents page; how much illustration will they include?
* Discuss which rules are most important. Ask children to say the rules aloud, as they would plan to write them. This means that the content has been established before the children begin to write.

When do two words become one?

Rewrite each speech bubble as two words.

Write the short forms for each of these:

Focus: understanding contractions

Crossword puzzle

Fill in the crossword.

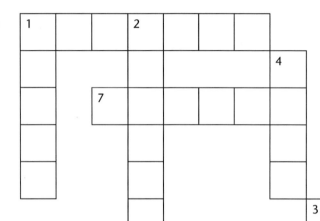

All these words are in *Earthling Study Skills*.
All the words are about school and learning.

Across

1 The boss in the classroom.
7 You must do this if you want to learn.
8 You can ask this.
9 Show this to yourself and to others.

Down

1 Teachers want to do this.
2 There are lots of these in school.
3 You can do this to a question.
4 If you learn something, you _ _ _ _ it.
5 Children like to do this.
6 You come to school to do this.

Use these words:

answer	learn	respect	teacher
children	listen	talk	teach
know	question		

Make a book of rules

Follow the instructions and make a book of rules for your classroom.

To make the book you will need:
- a pair of scissors
- a piece of paper
- coloured pens and pencils.

1. Fold the paper into eight rectangles.

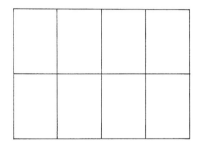

2. Fold the paper in half, then cut half way across the paper carefully like this.

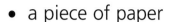
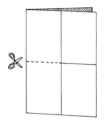

3. Fold the paper like this.

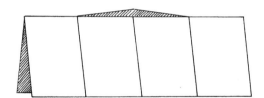

4. Push the left and right sides in to make a cube . . .

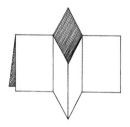

5. . . . then a cross.

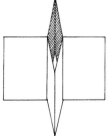

6. Fold the cover round to make the booklet.

7. Think about:
   a) a title for your book
   b) which rules to write
   c) which pictures you need to draw
   d) the blurb for your back cover.

You could use some of the rules in *Earthling Study Skills* if you want to.

Skeleton Clues

Author: Sarah Fleming
Genre: non-fiction   **Text type:** report
Pictures: illustrations and photographs

What can we learn from bones? Find out how much information scientists can learn from finding even one bone from an animal ... or even from a dinosaur.

Main information about the book

Total number of words: 153	Number of different words: 71
Total number of sentences: 16	Average sentence length: 9 words

Trackers high frequency words
a, and, are, at, big, but, can, find, from, have, how, in, is, like, look, of, on, one, out, that, the, these, they, to, use, we, what, which

'Tricky' words
chimpanzee, dinosaur, dolphin, family, human, skeleton, water

Words with consonant blends
and, dry, find, from, land, lots, must, past, skeleton, skull, under

Useful long vowel phonemes
'ue' in *clue, human, to, used* etc.
'ee' in *been, chimpanzee, eat, sea, teeth, these* etc.

Useful strategies
Splitting words into syllables, e.g. *chimp-an-zee, dol-phin*

Cross-curricular links

Science
★ Classification and adaptation – discussing ideas from the book can help children to understand different kinds of information we can use to find out how animals live and change.
★ Life processes and habitat – talk about how we can find out about how animals lived using evidence from their bones.

Geography
★ Patterns and processes – can children explain how skeletons and bones can provide evidence of geographical change?

History
★ Historical interpretation – discuss different kinds of historical artefacts, including bones. What can we learn from them?

ICT
★ Recording information – help children to understand how computer databases, digital photography etc. are invaluable tools of the modern scientist.

Linked PCMs

Word level work: (p.51) segmenting words into syllables
★ Check that the children know what a syllable is.
★ Read all the words on the PCM together. Ask the children to clap the syllables each time.
★ All these words are somewhere in the text. Can the children find them?

Reading for meaning: (p.52) finding information
★ Read the questions together.
★ Ask children to find the place in the book where each piece of information is given.
★ Can the children explain why we can't find all of this information from bones?

Writing: (p.53) writing glossary entries
★ Do the children know where to find the glossary, and what it is for?
★ Talk about the organisation (alphabetical).
★ Check that the children can read all of the words. Which are in the index?
★ Before the children write anything, encourage them to speak aloud the words that they plan to write, so the content is known before the children begin to write.

Broken bones

Write one syllable on each bit of bone.

The first one has been done for you.

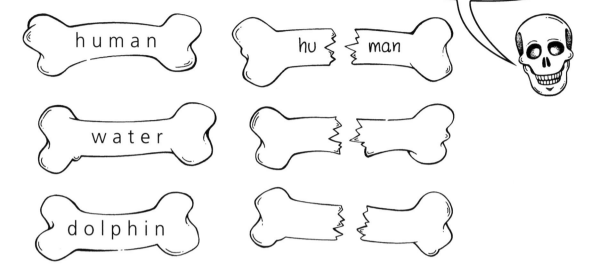

Write another 2 syllable word from the book on this bone.

Write one syllable on each bit of bone.

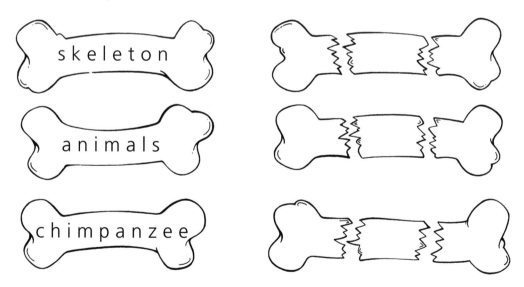

Write another 3 syllable word from the book on this bone.

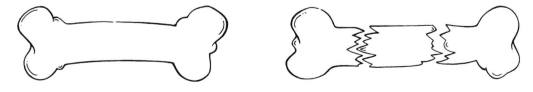

Focus: segmenting words into syllables

51

What can bones tell us?

Can we use bones to find out . . .

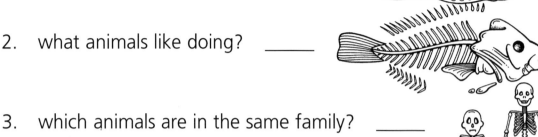

1. what animals eat?   <u>yes</u>

2. what animals like doing?   _____

3. which animals are in the same family?   _____

4. how much animals like to sleep?   _____

5. how big dinosaurs were?   _____

6. which colour dinosaurs were?   _____

7. which animals dinosaurs looked like?   _____

Write two more things
we can find out
from bones:

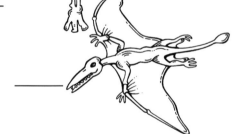

Draw your own picture clue from the book too.

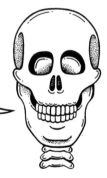

We can use bones to find out:

1. _____

2. _____

Focus: finding information

Understanding words

Ring the words that are in the glossary:

skeleton   dolphin

teeth   dinosaur

carnivore   human

dry land   (skull)

herbivore

Write your own glossary of definitions for the other words.

_____   _____

                              _____

_____   _____

                              _____

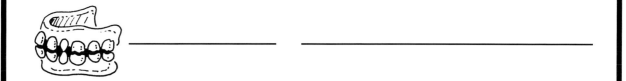

_____   _____

                              _____

_____   _____

                              _____

Pick Out a Person

> **Author:** Sarah Fleming
> **Genre:** non-fiction   **Text type:** puzzle
> **Pictures:** photographs

How carefully can you look? Can you pick out one person in a crowd? Test yourself against your friends. Who's the fastest?

Main information about the book

Total number of words: 232	Number of different words: 96
Total number of sentences: 14	Average sentence length: 15 words

Trackers **high frequency words**
a, and, big, can, find, in, is, no, of, on, out, the, what, who, with

'Tricky' words
catching, colour, jacket, photo, satellite, tongue, walking, water, woman

Words with consonant blends
blue, child, driver, flags, flowers, glasses, green, number, people, purple, step, stick, sunglasses, three, train, tray, watch

Useful long vowel phonemes
'or' in *ball, four, more, walking, water* etc.
'ir' in *person, purple, turn, word* etc.

Useful strategies
Making good use of keys and picture cues.

Cross-curricular links

Use different photographs as the basis for discussion about:

Geography
★ Geographical deductions about climate, landscape, physical and human features.
★ Culture – what expectations people in different cultures have, how they dress etc.

History
★ When the photographs were taken and how we know; why they might have been taken; differences between images shown in the photographs and more modern images.

Maths
★ Counting and estimation – discuss strategies using different photographs.
★ Categorisation – sort different elements in the photos using different criteria.
★ Data handling – discuss different ways of representing different aspects of each photo.
★ Co-ordinates – show the children how to use the grid in the Guided Reading Booklet to identify where everything is. Can they predict which square something will be in?

Linked PCMs

Word level work: (p.55) finding familiar letter patterns
★ Explain that knowing letter patterns is helpful for this activity – and also for spelling!
★ Reinforce that this activity is not about rearranging letters – the whole word is in each car.
★ Once children have found the words, ask them to explain how they know when to begin word building each time.

Reading for meaning: (p.56) finding information
★ Show children the co-ordinates grids in the Guided Reading Booklet. Explain that this activity is like that.
★ The children should read the questions and record the relevant square each time.

Writing: (p.57) writing a brief description
★ Revisit one of the pages and remind the children how the language structures work.
★ Can the children orally use those language structures to suggest particular penguins or features of the picture on the page?
★ Once children have decided what they plan to write, let them finish the activity.

Word hunt 1

Pick out the word in each car.

Do not try to use all the letters.

p x <u>p e r s o n</u> f t

l n u m b e r t y l

z x f f l a g s r n p

p h o t o r n s t l n

Find these words:

colour, flags, number, people, photo, water, year

r f t c o l o u r m n p

s y n p e o p l e p p t

e z r y e a r v v n p

u a w a t e r n u s l

Count the syllables in all the words you found.

Picture puzzle

Write the square where you can find each picture.

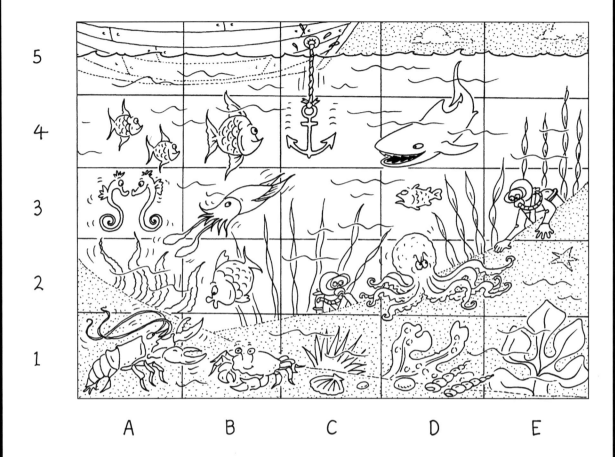

A B C D E

Key

octopus

anchor

crab

diver   sea horses   shark

1. The octopus is in square _____2D_____

2. The anchor is in square _____

3. The crab is in square _____

4. The divers are in squares _____

5. The sea horses are in square _____

6. The shark is in square _____

56

Focus: finding information

Pick out a penguin

Key

penguin

hat

scarf

skating

fishing

skiing

Look at the book to remind you what information to give your reader.

Write the questions.

 Can you see:

- _____

- _____

- _____

 Find:

- _____

- _____

- _____

A Week With the Fleets

> **Author:** Sarah Fleming
> **Genre:** non-fiction   **Text type:** puzzle
> **Pictures:** computer graphics

The Fleet Family is going on holiday. Use all the clues and information in the book to help to decide what they should do.

Main information about the book

Total number of words: 298   Number of different words: 147
Total number of sentences: 47   Average sentence length: 6 words

Trackers high frequency words
a, are, at, can, do, find, for, go, have, I, in, is, it, like, look, me, of, on, out, that, the, them, there, they, to, up, want, what, when, which, who, with, you, your

'Tricky' words
cheating, computer, front, groups, near, people, together, treasure

Words with consonant blends
and, drinks, first, Fleet, front, golden, granny, help, last, lost, people, plan, platform, play, salt, snails, stand, stuck, train, treasure

Useful long vowel phonemes
'ee' in *being, eat, cheating, Fleets, material, need, please, week* etc.
'ue' in *do, group, lose, new, room, together, too, who* etc

Useful strategies
Splitting words into syllables, e.g. *cheat-ing, gold-en, hol-i-day*

Cross-curricular links

Geography
★ Reading and interpreting maps and plans at different scales. Talk about the different purposes of each of the plans and maps – from house floor plan, to game plan to street map.
★ Recognising how physical characteristics affect human activities and behaviour. Discuss how the environment determines choices and decisions.

ICT
★ Graphic choices – talk about how the Fleets and their world are drawn on a computer. Why might an illustrator choose this approach?
★ Simulated worlds – discuss how computers can be used to construct simulated worlds and to explore 'what if' questions.

PSHCE
★ Group and family dynamics. How are decisions made in this family? Is it democratic? Is everybody's voice heard and considered?

Linked PCMs

Word level work: (p.59) counting phonemes
★ Check that the children know how to count the number of phonemes in a word.
★ Read the words on the left-hand side of the page, and draw in the phoneme buttons together. Then let the children find words with the same number of phonemes on the right-hand side.

Reading for meaning: (p.60) comprehension – who did what?
★ Read all the thought bubbles together. Ask who did what, and use the book to check.
★ Why are all the thought bubbles written in the past tense? In which tense are the words in the book?
★ If the children draw the characters, ask them to make the expression match the memory.

Writing: (p.61) instructions on how to play a game
★ Explain the task: to draw your own game similar to the one on pages 12 and 13.
★ Use the text on pages 12 and 13 as a model, but encourage the children to think of their own aim, reward(s) and danger(s). Ask them to draw and label items for the Key.

How many phonemes?

How many phonemes are there in each name?

Count the phoneme buttons.

J o e

T i m

L o l a

G r a n n y

Draw phoneme buttons to count the number of phonemes in each word.

   t r a i n

s h o p p i n g

   b o y s

g a r d e n

   s n a i l s

h o l i d a y

d r i n k s

r a c e

Then draw a line to join words with the same number of phonemes.

Look at pages 2 and 3 in the book.

Which word has most phonemes? _____

Which word has fewest? _____

What happened on holiday?

The Fleets are thinking about their holiday.
Draw who is thinking about what.

I wanted a TV in my bedroom.	I lost my snails.	I had to sleep in the same room as Tim.
I liked looking at the art.	I nearly sat on a snail.	I got stuck in a tunnel.

Which Fleet is missing? _____

What did he do on holiday? _____

Focus: comprehension – who did what?

Computer game

Make a new game for Tim to play.

Aim: _____

On the way _____

_____

_____

_____

_____

Key

Sand, Kippers or Aliens?

> **Author:** Sarah Fleming
> **Genre:** non-fiction   **Text type:** instruction (procedural)
> **Pictures:** illustrations and photographs

What do you do during indoor playtimes? This book gives ideas and instructions for three games you could play.

Main information about the book

Total number of words: 448	Number of different words: 171
Total number of sentences: 78	Average sentence length: 5 words

Trackers high frequency words
a, and, are, but, can, do, first, for, go, have, here, how, in, is, it, like, look, make, me, next, of, on, one, put, that, the, these, they, this, three, to, two, up, use, we, what's, when, with, you, your

'Tricky' words
alien, bored, coin, finally, finish, half, newspaper, points, ready, steady, scissors, who, whole, why

Words with consonant blends
blow, draw, end, fewest, floor, fold, kind, number, place, player, point, sand, spade, start, steady, stop, swim, throw, tray, try, want

Useful long vowel phonemes
'ai' in *aim, alien, away, later, paper, taking, wait, way* etc.
'ie' in *behind, dice, eye, finally, kind, line, my, try, why* etc.

Useful strategies
Splitting words into syllables, e.g. *news-pap-er, fin-al-ly, kip-per*

Cross-curricular links

Science
★ Materials and their properties – why do you need wet sand to make a sand pudding? Why should you make a kipper out of paper, not fabric?
★ Forces – discuss how the kipper is moved. Investigate how it can be moved faster – change the shape or size of the kipper? vary the force?

Maths
★ Data handling – explore different ways of keeping score as you play the games.
★ Probability – use two dice to play the aliens game, but you have to choose just one of the numbers to draw. Which should you choose?
★ Symmetry – explore different ways of making kippers and other creatures. Which can you make by simply folding the paper, and which must you cut out all round the shape?

PSHCE
★ Group relationships. Discuss turn taking, value of rules, fairness etc. How do these work? What are appropriate sanctions if people choose not to keep to the rules?

Linked PCMs

Word level work: (p.63) finding rhyming words
★ Children can do this activity independently, or playing against each other. When they find a rhyming word, they can draw part of their alien and write the word and page number in the box. Less confident children will benefit from keeping the word lists in view.

Reading for meaning: (p.64) finding information
★ Do children remember how each game is won? Ask them to re-read the book to find out. They should then draw lines joining the speech bubbles to the games and fill in the final box.

Writing: (p.65) writing brief instructions
★ All the information the children need can be found in the speech bubbles on pages 7 and 8. Encourage them to check spellings with the book.
★ Use this activity as an opportunity to explore the language of instructions. Does it make any difference if they are written down or spoken?

Words with the same sound

Draw an alien when you find the rhyming words in the book.

Draw a **head** when you find a word that rhymes with **OK**.

Draw a **body** when you find a word that rhymes with **aim**.

Draw a **tail** when you find a word that rhymes with **you**.

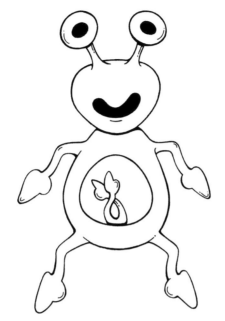

Draw an **eye** when you find a word that rhymes with **see**. (You need 2 of these.)

Draw a **mouth** when you find a word that rhymes with **throw**.

Draw a **leg** when you find a word that rhymes with **four**. (You need 4 of these.)

Draw your alien here.	Write the words you found here and the page number:		
	Word	**Rhymes with**	**Page**
		see	
		throw	
		four	
		OK	
		aim	
		you	

Fold your paper over here to hide the answers.

Find these words in the book to help you:

four, draw, your, before, for   you, to, two, too   aim, game
OK, play, way   see, be, me, we, three   throw, blow, go

Focus: finding rhyming words

Who is the winner?

How do you win each game?
Draw a line to match the game and the winner.

The kipper race

I had fewest points so I won.

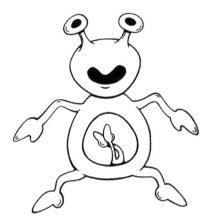

The alien race

My kipper got to the finish first, so I won.

Sand pudding

Finish the speech bubble.

Focus: finding information

How to make a Kipper

Read pages 7 and 8 in the book.
Write instructions for making a kipper to play the game.

How to make a Kipper for the Kipper Race

You will need:

a newspaper (for later)

_____

_____   _____

_____

_____

_____

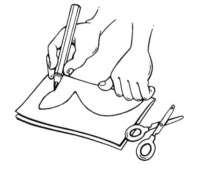

_____

_____

_____

_____

_____

_____

Focus: writing brief instructions

65

Eye Tricks

> **Author:** Sarah Fleming
> **Genre:** non-fiction **Text type:** instruction (procedural)
> **Pictures:** illustrations, photographs, computer graphics, paintings

Did you know you can trick your own eyes? Learn how to trick your eyes – and how to make simple tricks to play on your friends and parents.

Main information about the book

Total number of words: 441	Number of different words: 159
Total number of sentences: 36	Average sentence length: 12 words

Trackers high frequency words
a, and, are, at, big, can, for, from, here, how, in, is, it, look, make, many, of, on, one, that, the, them, then, there, these, they, this, to, two, up, use, what, will, with, you, your

'Tricky' words
beyond, circles, computer, diagonally, further, middle, parallel, picture, scissors, squared

Words with consonant blends
across, ask, bend, blue, brain, close, computer, draw, floating, friend, front, hands, hold, impossible, match, paste, pencil, point, prongs, simple, small, square, trace, trick

Useful long vowel phonemes
'ai' in *away, brain, make, page, paper, paste, same, trace* etc.
'ie' in *eye, like, line, side, sign, time, try, why, wide, write* etc

Useful strategies
Splitting words into syllables, e.g. *in-struc-tions, par-all-el, pen-cil*

Cross-curricular links

Art/Design and technology

★ Developing ideas – discuss what each of the artists whose work is reproduced might have been trying to achieve.
★ Starting points – what do you think the starting point was for each of these images?
★ Investigating tools and materials – discuss what media and tools each artist used, and consider why those choices were made.

ICT

★ Identifying patterns and exploring relationships and *what if* questions – why is ICT a good tool for making Eye Tricks?
★ Developing skills – encourage children to use the computer as suggested in the book.

Science

★ Seeing and thinking – help the children to relate what they know about how the eye works with this information about how the eye and brain work together.

Linked PCMs

Word level work: (p.67) sorting familiar letter patterns
★ Explain that knowing letter patterns is helpful for this activity – and also for spelling!
★ All the mixed-up words are found in the book.
★ Encourage those children who don't need the answers to fold them under and work without them.

Reading for meaning: (p.68) finding information
★ Ask children to find each of the three tricks shown in the book.
★ Can they explain why each kind of trick works?
★ Once the children have done the matching activity, let them draw an example of the remaining trick.

Writing: (p.69) writing brief explanations
★ Ask the children to find the first trick in the book and to read why it works. They should then close the book and explain in their own words before beginning to write.
★ See if the children can work out for themselves why the second trick works.

Word hunt 2

Work out the words and write them down.

The first letter has been underlined for each one

e
y   e   ——————————
s

n
m   y   ——————————
a

i   e
c   l   ——————————
n   p

r   o
l   o   ——————————
c   u

h   t
e   e   ——————————
s

r   c
k   s   ——————————
i   t

e   o
c   t   ——————————
r   m
u   p

p   e
r   c   ——————————
s   i
u   t

Put a circle round the words with more than 1 syllable.

Fold your paper over here to hide the answers.

- -

colour, computer, eyes, many,
pencil, pictures, these, tricks

Focus: sorting familiar letter patterns

How does it work?

Draw a line from the picture of each eye trick to the explanation of the way it works.

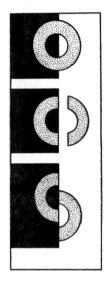

Look for these tricks in the book

What you read and what you see don't match.	Colours look different because of the colours around them.	Pictures trick our eyes because of what is close to them.	Parallel lines look like they bend because of what is around them.

12
ABC
14

Draw the last eye trick here.

Focus: finding information

Bigger? Longer?

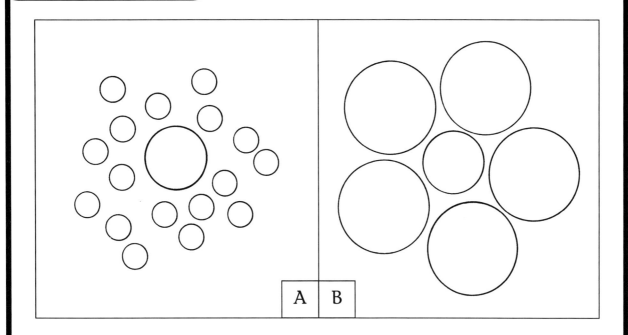

| A | B |

Which of the middle circles looks bigger (A or B)? _____

Why? _____

_____

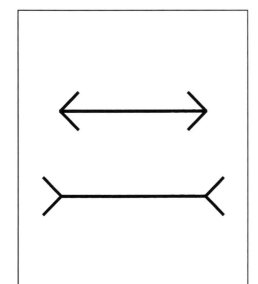

Which of these lines looks longer?

_____

Why do you think this is?

_____

_____

_____

Focus: writing brief explanations

69

Zero Gravity

> **Author:** Sarah Fleming
> **Genre:** non-fiction   **Text type:** report
> **Pictures:** illustrations and photographs

How is 'gravity' different from 'zero gravity'? Where do you find 'zero gravity'? How do you wash when the water doesn't fall down? The answers to all these questions … and more … are in this book.

Main information about the book

Total number of words: 211   Number of different words: 106
Total number of sentences: 26   Average sentence length: 8 words

Trackers high frequency words
a, and, at, back, can, do, first, go, have, here, in, is, it, like, make, no, of, on, one, them, there, this, three, to, two, up, use, we, when, which, will, you

'Tricky' words
astronaut, blood, discovered, experiments, force, gravity, muscles, Newton, pencil, sickness, suction, toilet, usually, vacuum cleaner

Words with consonant blends
blood, cleaner, experiments, gravity, help, pencil, small, space, soft, stay, strong, strange

Useful long vowel phonemes
'oa' in *almost, astronaut, bones, don't, goes, micro, no, zero* etc.
'ai' in *change, day, makes, space, strange, take, way* etc.

Useful strategies
Splitting words into syllables, e.g. *ex-per-i-ment, grav-i-ty, sick-ness*

Cross-curricular links

Science
* ★ Forces – understanding gravity, zero gravity and suction.
* ★ Life processes – understanding how zero gravity and gravity affect the human body.
* ★ Scientific enquiry – understanding that conditions in zero gravity are different and exploring ways of finding out how.

Geography
* ★ Earth and beyond – understanding the place of earth in space and how earth and space differ.

Linked PCMs

Word level work: (p.71) counting syllables
* ★ Check that the children know what a syllable is.
* ★ Read all the words on the PCM together. Ask the children to clap the syllables each time.

* ★ All these words are somewhere in the text. Can the children find them?

Reading for meaning: (p.72) finding information
* ★ Check that the children know the conventions of crosswords, including that words can be written from left to right or from top to bottom, and the conventions of numbering crosswords.
* ★ As they read each definition, ask them to check with the word list at the bottom to find the answer.
* ★ Can they find all these words in the book?

Writing: (p.73) recording information using the book and personal experience
* ★ Check that the children can explain the difference between zero gravity and gravity on earth.
* ★ Ask each child to read one of the activities at the bottom and explain why it would be easier or harder in zero gravity.

Count the syllables

Re-read the words. Underline each syllable in a different colour.

g r a v i t y

e a r t h

s p a c e s h i p

b o o k

s p a c e

t h r e e

t o i l e t

a s t r o n a u t

Write each of the words in a spaceship.

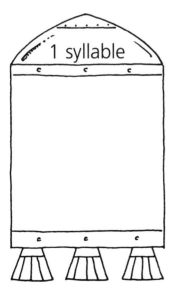

1 syllable

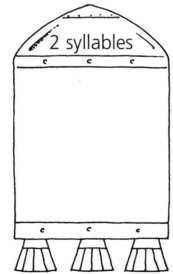

2 syllables

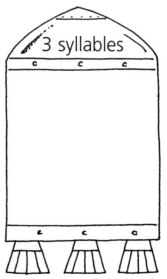

3 syllables

Add two more words from the book to each spaceship.

Zero Gravity crossword

Fill in the crossword.

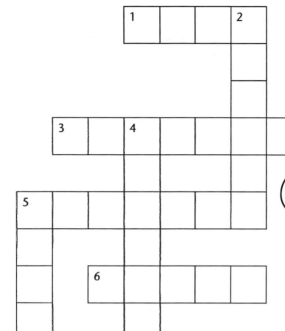

All the words are in *Zero Gravity*.

Across

1 Gravity pulls things _ _ _ _.

3 The force that pulls you towards VERY big things.

5 You use this to make a pulling force in a spaceship.

6 Gravity is a _ _ _ _ _.

7 You go into space in one of these.

Down

2 He discovered gravity.

4 A person who goes into space.

5 Your bones go like this in space.

Use these words:
astronaut down force gravity
Newton soft spaceship suction

Focus: finding information

What can you do in zero gravity?

What would it be hard to do in zero gravity? What would be easy?

In zero gravity
it would be HARD to...

In zero gravity
it would be EASY to...

Think about these things:

jump up high

get dressed

sleep

lift something

catch a ball

write

read a book

drink from a cup

dance

Add more ideas of your own.

Level 1: Elephant tracks – fiction

> **Author:** Paul Shipton
> **Illustrator:** David Mostyn

The Big Mess

Nick arrives at his new school on Planet Zap and quickly makes friends (and enemies).
He offers a crisp to one of his new friends, and that's when the trouble begins.

Total number of words: 259	Number of different words: 100
Total number of sentences: 51	Average sentence length: 5 words

Trackers high frequency words
a, and, asked, at, back, big, but, can, didn't, he, here, I, in, is, it, like, look, me, next, no, of, on, out, put, said, that, the, to, up, was, went, will, with

'Tricky' words
classroom, doesn't, don't, lunchtime, Mant, new, school, teacher

Words with consonant blends
Blop, crisp(s), drop, dump, just, last, lunch, Plop, Slig, slot, snack, stop, watch

Useful strategies
Understanding contractions, e.g. *didn't, don't, he's, it's, what's*

PCM 1 (p.78) recognising consonant blends at the beginnings and ends of words
★ Look at all the consonant blends. Can the children tell which can only be a word ending or a word beginning?
★ Each consonant blend should only be used once.

PCM 2 (p.79) sequencing events in the story
★ Can the children tell you which order these events occurred in? Check with the book.
★ Once the children have sequenced the pictures, ask them to retell the story, using the pictures as prompts.

Buzz Ball

Jax is better than Slig at Buzz Ball and Slig is unhappy. His friends decide to help him . . .

Total number of words: 253	Number of different words: 89
Total number of sentences: 47	Average sentence length: 5 words

Trackers high frequency words
a, and, asked, but, he, I, in, is, it, like, look, next, no, on, put, said, that, the, this, to, up, was, we, went, what, will, with, you

'Tricky' words
lunchtime, playtime, school, something, why

Words with consonant blends
fast, Glitch, grin, lost, pack, play, stop, strong, switched, switching, twit

Useful strategies
Compound words, e.g. *lunch + time, play + time, some + thing*

PCM 1 (p.80) counting phonemes
★ Check that the children understand the difference between 'phoneme' (or sound) and letter. Remind them about using 'phoneme buttons' to show how many phonemes there are in a word.
★ Can they find four letter words with one or two phonemes? (e.g. bear, fair)

PCM 2 (p.81) working out which character did what
★ Check that the children understand the task, which is to join each speech bubble to the correct character.
★ Point out that all the speech bubbles are in the first person ('I'). Can the children find the comparable sentence in the book?

Catch it, Tizz!

Slig makes fun of Tizz because Tizz isn't good at catching. But can Tizz catch when it's really important?

Total number of words: 241	Number of different words: 92
Total number of sentences: 48	Average sentence length: 5 words

Trackers high frequency words
a, and, are, asked, at, back, but, can, didn't, do, he, here, I, in, is, it, like, look, make, next, no, of, on, out, said, that, the, then, this, to, was, we, went

'Tricky' words
lesson, school, switched, teacher, wasn't

Words with consonant blends
best, Blop, catch, clank, crash, fast, Glitch, help, jumped, quick, smash

Useful strategies
Understanding contractions, e.g. *can't, didn't, it's, wasn't, where's*

PCM 1 (p.82) recognising contractions
* ★ Read the top sentence on the PCM. Talk about *can't*. Do the children recognise it as a contraction of *can* + *not*? Discuss how the apostrophe represents the missing letters.

PCM 2 (p.83) understanding the story
* ★ Check that the children understand the terms 'true' and 'false'.
* ★ Read the first sentence together and agree whether it is true or false. How do the children know?

The Duck from Zog

Jen and Nick have a new pet. It's a duck from Zog, and it's not like other ducks.

Total number of words: 194	Number of different words: 76
Total number of sentences: 32	Average sentence length: 6 words

Trackers high frequency words
a, after, and, asked, at, back, big, but, can, didn't, do, fast, he, here, I, is, it, like, look, no, of, on, one, out, said, the, then, this, to, up, was, we, went

'Tricky' words
come, why

Words with consonant blends
catch, crisp(s), croc, duck, fetch, from, help, jump, last, play, stick, trick(s)

Useful strategies
Recognition of -ed endings, e.g. *asked, jumped, looked, picked*

PCM 1 (p.84) combining syllables to make new animal names
* ★ Can the children use the word sum at the top of the page to explain how the 'crocdog' got its name? If possible, refer to an illustration in the book and define the features of both crocodile and dog.
* ★ Ask the children to suggest animal outcomes from combining one syllable from each name in the other word sums. The order of the syllables in the answer doesn't matter (i.e. *catphant* and *elecat* are both acceptable).

* ★ Ask the children to draw their new creatures, combining characteristics from both.

PCM 2 (p.85) recognising a character's reactions to events in the story
* ★ Read each of the extracts together and ask the children to tell you what they think was the Duck's reaction each time. Check in the book.
* ★ Ask the children to describe the character of the Duck. Is it a good pet? Why?

Level 2: Frog tracks – fiction

Author: Paul Shipton
Illustrator: David Mostyn

Big Bad Slig

Oh oh! Slig has a new machine. This can't be good news for Nick and his friends ...

Total number of words: 265	Number of different words: 108
Total number of sentences: 37	Average sentence length: 7 words

Trackers high frequency words
a, and, are, asked, at, big, but, can, go(ing), he, how, I, in, it, just, look, make, me, next, of, on, out, put, said, the, them, then, they, this, three, to, up, very, was, we, what, when

'Tricky' words
afraid, cupboard, eight, laughing, machine, shrink

Words with consonant blends and useful long vowel phonemes
afraid, bent, Blop, class, cross, friends, Glitch, grow, just, little, must, next, plan, shrink, Slig, spider, stuck, test, three
'ow' in about, how, out etc.; 'ai' in afraid, came, eight, made, make, they

Useful strategies
Common word endings, e.g. *laugh-ing, friend-s, push-ed*

***PCM 1** (p.86) recognising contractions*
★ Can the children tell you what they normally say instead of *did not* or *can not*? Remind them of the role of the apostrophe in contractions.
★ Do the children know the full forms of the contractions on the second half of the sheet?

***PCM 2** (p.87) understanding characters*
★ Ask the children to use the page references to find out what colour Rex is in each picture. Establish that Rex's colour reflects his feelings. How do they think he feels in each picture?
★ They can use this information to complete the table at the bottom of the page.

The Copy Cat

Copy Cats on Planet Zap look a bit like Earth cats, but they can do things that no Earth cat can do ...

Total number of words: 332	Number of different words: 108
Total number of sentences: 46	Average sentence length: 7 words

Trackers high frequency words
a, and, back, but, can, didn't, do, for, from, front, he, I, in, is, it, just, look, me, no, of, one, out, said, that, the, them, then, there, they, this, up, was, went, what, when, who, with

'Tricky' words
afraid, classroom, front, person, school, smashed, threw, waited, walked, water

Words with consonant blends and useful long vowel phonemes
afraid, classroom, children, front, grin, lots, past, school, smashed, told, window
'or' in all, fall, moral, saw, walked, water etc.; 'ai' in afraid, made, they, waited etc.

Useful strategies
Common word endings, e.g. *jump-ed, thing-s*

***PCM 1** (p.88) doubling consonants before adding -ing or -ed*
★ Check children already know that when a short vowel is followed by one consonant, that consonant is doubled before *-ing* or *-ed*.
★ Children should tick the copy cat picture if they need to double the final consonant and put a cross through it if they don't.

***PCM 2** (p.89) finding the setting*
★ Ask children to find the pictures in the book. Where did each of these events take place?
★ Once children have stuck the place flashes on the sheet, ask them to talk about what happened next. Once they have made it clear that they understand how the story developed, they can complete the task.

Trackers level 2: Frog tracks

Just Like On Earth

Nick misses his home on Earth, so his friends ask Mr Potts to help them to have an Earth party for him. Mr Potts is *nearly* right about what happens at an Earth party.

Total number of words: 223	Number of different words: 106
Total number of sentences: 37	Average sentence length: 6 words

Trackers high frequency words
a, and, are, at, big, but, can, didn't, do, for, go(ing), he, have, I, in, is, it, just, like, look, next, no, of, on, put, said, that, the, there, they, to, up, very, want, was, we, went, with

'Tricky' words
balloon, Earth, fizzy, friends, parties, pulled

Words with consonant blends and useful long vowel phonemes
asked, bent, best, Blop, class, drinks, friends, Glitch, held, help, jump, just, landed, lots, people, play, wanted
'oa' in *don't, home, ok, rope* etc.; 'ar' in *(asked, class), party, parties*

Useful strategies
Common word endings, e.g. *drink-s, part-ies, land-ed*

PCM 1 (p.90) recognising plural endings
★ Check that the children understand the concept of 'plural' and that they know that the most common ways of making plurals are: adding *-s* (*cats, dogs, balloons*); adding *-es* (*foxes, dishes, classes*); changing *y* to *i* and adding *es*.

PCM 2 (p.91) explaining details in the setting
★ Discuss the picture on page 6, making sure the children understand that Mr Potts so often gets things *nearly* right, but not *quite* right. Ask the children to explain clearly what is wrong with the picture (focus on Mr Pott's clothing as well as on the food).
★ Find the images on the PCM in the picture. Ask the children to explain clearly what is wrong with each of the images. Then they can begin to write their explanations.

Getting on the Team

Nick wants to be on the school Buzz Ball team. But is he good enough?

Total number of words: 245	Number of different words: 114
Total number of sentences: 34	Average sentence length: 7 words

Trackers high frequency words
a, and, at, but, can, didn't, do, first, for, go(ing), he, I, in, it, just, like, me, next, of, on, out, said, the, then, there, this, to, very, want, was, went, with

'Tricky' words
children, friends, Mr, pitch, school, turn, won't

Words with consonant blends and useful long vowel phonemes
best, Block, children, crash, dreams, drop, fast, flew, Friday, friends, hands, help, just, last, most, pitch, play, school, Slig, still, stop, test, think, try, watch
'ee' in *be, dreams, he, me, she, team* etc.; 'ir' in *earth, first, turn, were* etc.

Useful strategies
Understanding apostrophes for possession, e.g. *Slig's, Tizz's*; and contraction, e.g. *it's, there's*

PCM 1 (p.92) recognising common word endings
★ Can children suggest a word ending with each of the endings written on the goals? What do they know about these endings?
★ Ask each of the children to pick one of the words and decide how many of the nets it could be written in.

PCM 2 (p.93): understanding characters
★ Ask the children to think about the story, without reference to the book. Can they tell you when Nick was happy or sad? When Slig was happy or sad? Let them look through the book to confirm their ideas.
★ As the children complete the activity, warn them to think about the use of the pronoun *he*. They should always read the complete sentence (e.g. *Nick was happy when he got on the team*) to work out who he refers to each time!

Mess is bad

Join the lost letters to the bits of words.

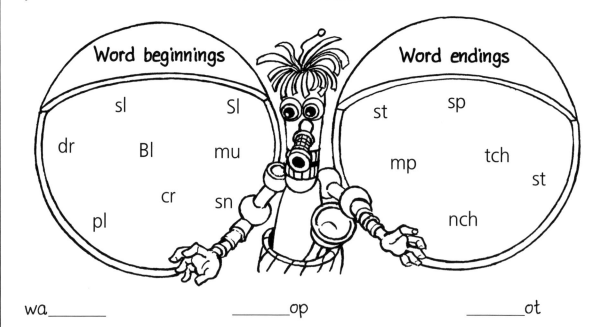

Word beginnings

sl   Sl
dr   Bl   mu
cr   sn
pl

Word endings

st   sp
mp   tch
st
nch

wa_____   _____op   _____ot

du_____   _____isp

ju_____   _____st

ju_____   _____op

lu_____   _____op   _____ig

cri_____   _____ack

How many of these words can you find in the book?

Focus: recognising consonant blends at the beginnings and ends of words

A very big mess

Put these events in order.

6 What happened next?
Write or draw in this box.

Phoneme goals

There are 4 letters in each of these words, but how many
phonemes are there?

Draw phoneme buttons like this:

N i c k   S l i g

Show which goal they go in.

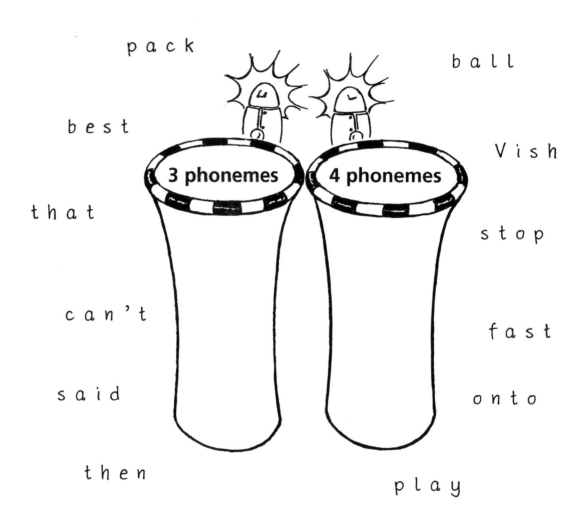

B u z z

g o o d

p a c k

b a l l

b e s t

V i s h

that

stop

c a n ' t

f a s t

s a i d

o n t o

t h e n

p l a y

3 phonemes   4 phonemes

Find other words with 4 letters and write them down.

_____   _____   _____

_____   _____   _____

What is the smallest number of phonemes you can count in
them? _____

Focus: counting phonemes

Who did what?

Draw a line to join the speech bubble to the right speaker.

I won the game of Buzz Ball.

I put something in Kaz's jet pack.

I put Slig's tag onto Kaz's jet pack and then I put Kaz's tag onto Slig's jet pack.

I watched Lug and Glitch at the end.

Write in the speech bubble to show what Slig did.

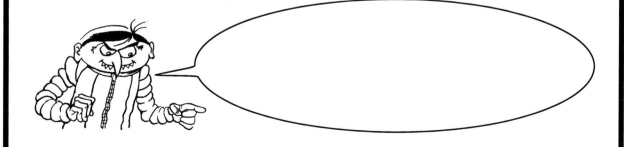

Word sums

Word sums

Tizz can't catch, but he can do sums.
Help him to complete these word sums.

did + _____ = didn't

_____ + not = wasn't

can + not = _____

where + _____ = where's

_____ + is = it's

you + are = _____

Use these words:
you're   is
not   it
was   can't

Make up some words of your own.

_____ + _____ = _____

_____ + _____ = _____

_____ + _____ = _____

_____ + _____ = _____

Use these words:
could   we're
she   am
not   she's
I   are
is   couldn't   I'm
we

Focus: recognising contractions

True or false?

Read the sentences.
Are they true or false?

	True	False
Tizz was good at P.E.	___	✓
Slig gave Tizz a pen.	___	___
Tizz liked robotics lessons.	___	___
The teacher made a Bug.	___	___
Slig made a good Bug.	___	___
Nick's Bug was fast.	___	___
Kaz could catch Nick's Bug.	___	___
Slig pushed Nick's Bug out of the window.	___	___
Nick's Bug crashed.	___	___
Tizz could catch Nick's Bug.	___	___

Write two more <u>true</u> sentences about the story.

_____

_____

_____

_____

Focus: understanding the story

83

Make an animal

crocodile   +   dog   =   crocdog

Which other animals can you make?

elephant   +   cat   =

tiger   +   mouse   =

camel   +   frog   =

hippo   +   bear   =

parrot   +   fish   =

Can you think of two more animals to join?

_____   +   _____   =

_____   +   _____   =

Focus: combining syllables to make new animal names

What did the duck do?

Cut out the pictures of the duck.
Which picture follows each event in the story?
Stick a picture in each box.

"Can it run?" asked Nick.	
The duck looked at Nick's crisps. Then it jumped up.	
"It's a Croc Dog!" said Jen. "Run!"	
What happened before the last picture? Write your sentence here. _____ _____	

Focus: recognising a character's reactions to events in the story

One word or two?

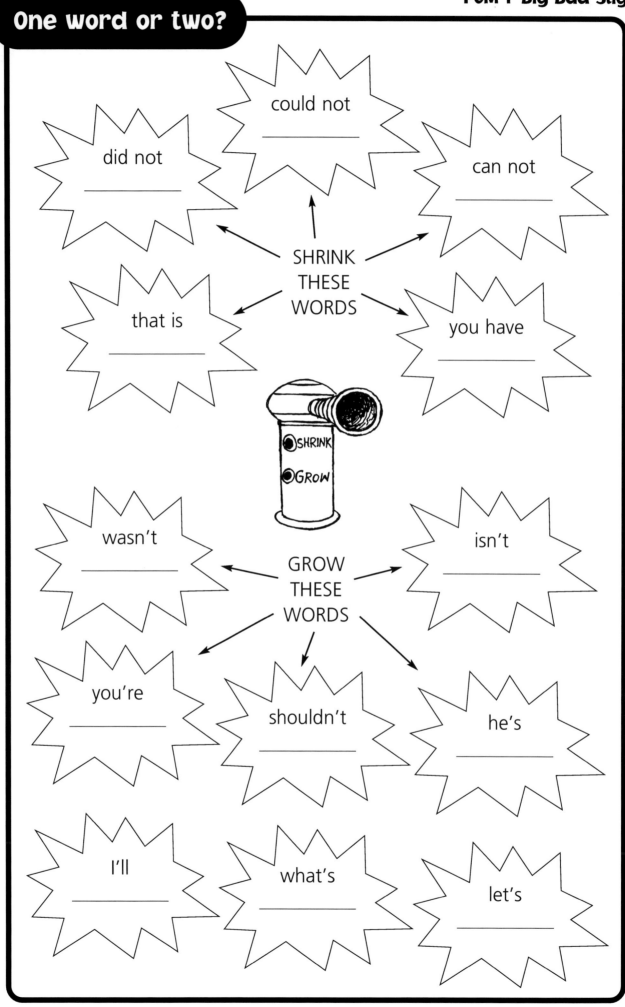

could not

did not

can not

SHRINK
THESE
WORDS

that is

you have

SHRINK

GROW

wasn't

isn't

GROW
THESE
WORDS

you're

shouldn't

he's

I'll

what's

let's

Focus: recognising contractions

How does Rex feel?

What colour is Rex in each of the pictures?

on page 3

on page 4

on page 10

on page 11

on page 13

on page 16

How does Rex feel in each picture?
Finish the sentences:

When Rex is afraid, he turns _____.

When Rex is _____ he turns _____.

When Rex is _____ he turns _____.

When Rex is _____ he turns _____.

Focus: understanding characters

Copycat consonants?

Write the answers to the word sums.
Do we need to copy the consonant before we add
the *-ing* or *-ed* ending?

run + ing = running   jump + ed = jumped

look + ing = _____

spin + ing = _____

walk + ed = _____

pull + ed = _____

smash + ing = _____

pick + ed = _____

wait + ing = _____

hop + ed = _____

Focus: doubling consonants before adding -ing or -ed

Where did it happen?

Cut out the boxes at the bottom of the page and stick them on the right pictures.
Then sequence the pictures to tell the story.

back in the classroom

Draw or write what happened next.

in the classroom

in the school

before school

in the corridor

Focus: finding the setting

More than one

How do you write 'more than one'?
Choose which ending to add to each word.

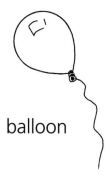 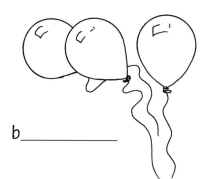 

balloon   b_____   es

glass   g_____   s

party   p_____   ies

What do you call more than one . . .

child?   _____

person?   _____

man?   _____

Focus: recognising plural endings

Party food?

What's wrong with the party food on pages 7 and 8?

Ice cream shouldn't _____

_____

Jam sandwiches shouldn't _____

_____

Hot dogs shouldn't _____

_____

Chocolate logs shouldn't_____

_____

Word endings

Which ending can you add to each word?
Write the new word in the right goal.

Use these words:
play   dream   hand   friend   net   school   want
thing   think   pick   turn   watch   pitch

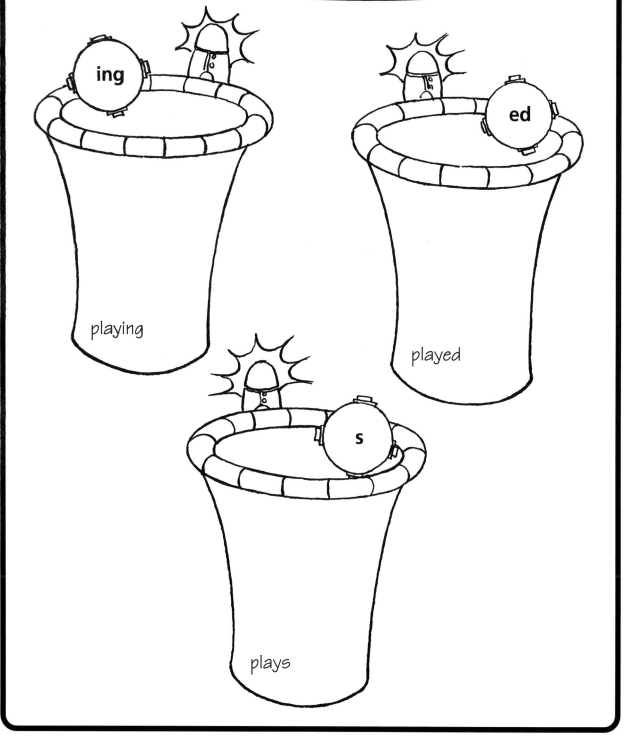

ing

playing

ed

played

s

plays

Focus: recognising common word endings

Happy or sad?

When were they happy or sad?

Nick was happy when . . .   Nick was sad when . . .

Slig was happy when . . .   Slig was sad when . . .

Cut out the boxes and stick them under the pictures . . .

Nick dropped the ball.	he didn't get on the team.
Nick got on the team.	he got on the team.

Focus: understanding characters

Using *Trackers* in guided reading

Guided reading

This is the term used to describe a session in which an adult works for about 20–25 minutes with a group of up to six children, all reading the same book.

A guided reading session should have four distinct parts:

- Introduction (2–3 minutes)
- Independent reading with a purpose (10–12 minutes)
- Returning to the text (5–6 minutes)
- Conclusion (2–3 minutes).

The Guided Reading Booklet for each individual *Trackers* book has more detailed suggestions, but this leaflet aims to explain the purpose of each part of the guided reading session and to offer ideas for good practice during the session.

Introduction

This may vary according to whether this is the first session with the book or a follow-up session.

In the **first session**, the purpose is to introduce the book.

- Identify the teaching and learning objectives of the session.
- Introduce the book by:
  - using title, blurb and cover illustrations to predict the subject matter and text type;
  - finding out what children already know about the subject.
- Remind children of recently introduced reading strategies.
- Agree on questions to be resolved during independent reading.

Asking and answering questions

There is a real skill to asking and answering questions in order to establish the child's true understanding both of the subject matter they are reading and of the reading strategies. There are two basic question types:

Closed questions are questions to which there is only one correct answer. An example might be: *Which planet is nearest to the sun? What sound does 'dog' begin with?*

Closed questions can be used to check whether or not a child knows or has found out a certain 'fact', but they don't usually show whether or not a child has understood something.

Open questions are questions to which there are many possible answers. Examples are questions which begin: *Why do you think . . .? In your opinion . . .? How would you . . .?*

Open questions are much better for assessing how much a child understands. They are also useful starting points for discussion, because different children may have different opinions.

Children asking questions

Encourage children to ask questions. By asking questions, children can begin to feel a sense of ownership of their own knowledge and understanding, and it gives them more control over what they need to know. Useful strategies in answering children's questions include:

- giving the child an opportunity to phrase the question accurately;
- when possible, encouraging other children to answer the questions;
- asking the questioner what s/he thinks may be the answer;
- trying to answer the question in a way that relates to the child's existing knowledge.

In the **follow-up session**, the purpose of the introduction is to re-focus the children on the book and to establish questions for further discussion.

- Identify the teaching objective of the session.
- Ask the children what they remember about the book from the previous session. Ask them to find parts of the text that gave specific information.
- Recall recently introduced reading strategies (e.g. *What can you do if you get stuck on a word? What should you do if you know that you have lost the sense of the passage?*).
- Identify points of possible difficulty (e.g. *Can you all find the word at the beginning of page 5? How could we work out what the word says?*). Many of these possible 'tricky' words are identified in the Guided Reading Booklet for the individual books.
- Agree on questions that the children are going to resolve during the independent reading part of the session. These are often suggested in the Guided Reading Booklet.

Independent reading

In this part of the session, the children should read the specified section of the book and try to resolve the agreed questions. As far as possible, the children should be encouraged to work independently. Meanwhile you can:

- sample the children's reading by listening carefully to short passages read by each one. Make careful use of specific praise, e.g. for strategies chosen or for phrasing and fluency;
- support individual readers (who are struggling) using selected prompts, if possible making reference to reading strategies discussed earlier.

Returning to the text

This is an important part of the session, because it is here that you can establish what the children understood from their reading. Use it to:

- ask the whole group if they were aware of any problems they encountered. Encourage group involvement in solving the problem;
- agree answers to the questions posed earlier;
- ask children to summarise what they have read;
- ask children to explain reading strategies they used and praise their use of emerging strategies;
- ask additional questions to prompt successful problem-solving strategies (e.g. *How did you know how to say this word? How did you decide which bit of the text was important to read?*);
- ask further questions to probe more deeply into the children's understanding of what they read;
- demonstrate effective reading by re-reading a section of the text yourself.

Conclusion

This part of the session can be used to:

- ask for personal responses to the text (e.g. *What do you remember best? Which bit interested you the most?*);
- establish questions for a future session with the same *Trackers* book;
- summarise the reading strategies that have been effective;
- return to the teaching and learning objectives to establish whether they have been achieved.

Reading profile for *Elephant tracks* and *Frog tracks*

Child's name_____   Assessment date _____

Home language _____   Date of birth _____

Reading for meaning
Elephant tracks
- expects the text to make sense?   YES/ NO
- predicts a word using syntactic cues?   YES/ NO
- predicts a word using picture cues?   YES/ NO
- has a general sense of 'what has been read so far'?   YES/ NO
- expresses an opinion about what has been read?   YES/ NO

Frog tracks
- is aware of an unrecognised word and hesitates?   YES/ NO
- is aware when meaning has been lost?   YES/ NO
- re-reads familiar text independently?   YES/ NO
- uses pictures to add detail and gain meaning?   YES/ NO

Reading for information
Elephant tracks
- predicts the contents of a book using cover information?   YES/ NO
- can talk about prior knowledge of the main topic in a non-fiction book?   YES/ NO
- uses pictures for information?   YES/ NO

Frog tracks
- with help, uses contents page and index to find information?   YES/ NO
- can identify different purposes of text (main text, captions, labels etc.)
  in a non-fiction book?   YES/ NO
- recognises a change of topic when reading?   YES/ NO

Phonic skills
Elephant tracks
- reads and writes CVC words?   YES/ NO
- uses phonic knowledge to recognise an initial letter?   YES/ NO
- makes accurate and consistent use of letter sounds to confirm words?   YES/ NO

Frog tracks
- consistently reads initial consonant blends?   YES/ NO
- consistently reads final consonant blends?   YES/ NO
- blends consonants and short vowel phonemes together to decode words?   YES/ NO
- recognises common word endings (-ing, -ed etc.)   YES/ NO

High frequency words
Elephant tracks

• 50 words	YES/ NO	* 60 words	YES/ NO	* 75 words	YES/ NO

Frog tracks

• 65 words	YES/ NO	* 110 words	YES/ NO	* 130+ words	YES/ NO

- recognises high frequency words in running text?   YES/ NO
- shows awareness of patterns in words?   YES/ NO